LANCASHIRE COTTON SPINNERS

LANCASHIRE COTTON SPINNERS

A fortune made in the mills

BY

WILLIAM M. HARTLEY

Also by the Author

The Hartleys: No Longer Shopkeepers – a Hartley Family progression

ISBN 978-1-904244-51-6

The Mellodews of Moorside: An Oldham Velvet Dynasty

ISBN 978-1-874181-64-4

Lancashire Cotton Spinners: A fortune made in the mills

First published in 2016
by Palatine Books,
Carnegie House,
Chatsworth Road
Lancaster LA1 4SL
www.palatinebooks.com

Copyright © William M. Hartley

British Library Cataloguing-in-Publication data
A catalogue record for this book is available from the British Library
Paperback ISBN 13: 978-1-910837-06-1

Designed and typeset by Carnegie Book Production
www.carnegiebookproduction.com
Printed and bound in Great Britain by TJ International Ltd,
Padstow, Cornwall

Contents

Preface and Acknowledgements

THIS BOOK ILLUSTRATES HOW three families – the Mannocks, Prockters and Holdens – after a humble start, combined their business interests. This combination was to provide a comfortable lifestyle for the next two generations during the first and second quarters of the twentieth century. This was helped by an astute change of investment so that the family did not experience the losses suffered by so many of their contemporaries during the 1930s.

The firm of Kirkham & Mannock Limited was a cotton spinning business based in Oldham at Marsland Mills. It was to close in 1959 after almost a century of trading. Its sister company, Prockter & Co. Limited, had closed some two decades earlier. These two companies were the key to the families' prosperity.

In September 2009 I was at the 100th birthday party of Mrs Alice Ramage, whose mother was a Holden and a granddaughter of Mr William Mannock. My book *An Oldham Velvet Dynasty – the Mellodews of Moorside* was about to be published. A fellow guest at the party, Barbara Brady (née Holden) hearing that I had been involved in looking at the cotton business of Oldham, sparked my interest when she said that she had papers relating to her family's business of Kirkham & Mannock in the attic of her house in Kensington. I was invited to visit, and did so.

I was attracted by the idea of looking at another family whose fortune had been made in the cotton trade. Whilst the Mellodews had been cotton spinners and manufacturers (in their case producing velvets, corduroy and similar fabrics) Barbara Brady's family, the Holdens, had limited their business to cotton spinning alone.

My first look at the papers kindly produced by Barbara Brady showed that there was little information about Kirkham & Mannock but there was information about the family's finances. My initial reaction to these papers suggested that an apt title for this book should be 'An Unremarkable Family'. This was not a family that had left its mark upon the Oldham 'stage'; it had not endowed civic buildings, it had not produced Mayors of Oldham, it had not patented inventions, it had not produced progeny that caused a stir.

Further research however made me realise that this title would be unfair. There is not a lot that can be found out about the business of Kirkham & Mannock, but what is remarkable is that, in spite of difficult trading times for the cotton industry in the second quarter of the twentieth century, the Holdens ran a business that continued to pay dividends, they held on to their desirable but modest fortune, when so many were losing theirs, and they continued to enjoy a comfortable way of life which would be the envy of many.

This book will look at how they achieved this state of affairs, how they consolidated their interests, how they were helped by judicious marriages and, ultimately, how they ceased to be connected with Oldham.

I could not have written this book without the papers produced by Barbara Brady, and I am most grateful to her for allowing me the use of them. My thanks must also go to the late Mrs Alice Ramage for describing family life in the 1920s and 1930s and to Shelagh Turner-Jones (the widow of John Vernon Holden) for further papers and background material.

My earlier book – *An Oldham Velvet Dynasty – the Mellodews of Moorside* (ISBN 978-1-874181-64-4) – made use of papers lent to me by Nicky and Michael Hawley. Once again, I thank them for allowing me to make use of these papers, which give details of the Holden Trusts from which Alice Maud Mellodew (née Holden) received benefit.

Barbara Brady's papers revealed the importance of a Holden marriage to the daughter of Isaac Prockter. This led me to Bartholomew Prockter and the enormous family tree that descended from him, revealing two marriages into the family of James Stott, another Oldham entrepreneurial cotton spinner and manufacturer.

The connection was too important to be ignored. Subsequent research led me to Jenny Stott and her cousin James Stott, to their papers and their knowledge of the Stott family. I am most grateful to them for their time and loan, in particular, of a book of reminiscences about the original James Stott.

The staff of the Oldham Local Studies and Archives have been most helpful and showed their usual unfailing courtesy. Joanna Robson (Archive Officer) Roger Ivens (Local Studies Officer) and Sean Baggaley (Exhibitions and Collections Co-ordinator, Social History Collection at Gallery Oldham) provided information and images with enthusiasm. Photographer Margaret Davison was good enough to provide some of the photographs for the illustrations, taken on a damp and dismal Oldham day. Jane Marchent used her skill of perusing detail in correcting obvious errors. I am grateful to all of them for their help.

I have been lucky enough to be able to rely upon original documents, but where I have had to make assumptions, I can only hope that they are correct. If not, I can only apologise to those affected.

Alderley Edge, Cheshire.
September 2016

Background

Lthough Oldham, some seven miles north east of Manchester, was not insignificant in size at the beginning of the nineteenth century, with a population in 1801 of 12,204, it grew rapidly as its original hatting trade was fast superseded by cotton spinning. By 1811 it had a population of 16,930, rising to 21,662 in 1821 and to 72,333 by 1861. Its population would more than double to 147,483 by 1911.

In 1849 the *Morning Chronicle*'s reporter Angus Bethune Reach was sent to report on Manchester and the surrounding textile districts. He described Oldham as 'a mean looking straggling town … shabby … houses filthy and smouldering, airless little back streets, dismal waste ground … with melancholy clusters of gaunt, dirty, unshaven men lounging on the pavement.'

This description does not recognise the great activity that was taking place in Oldham.

By the mid-nineteenth century there was a growing English middle class with an appetite for cotton goods. There was similar demand from abroad, especially India and the Far East. In 1800 cotton weighing 56 million pounds was consumed in British mills. By 1830 this had risen to 263 million pounds and by 1840 to 572 million pounds. This indicates the scale of demand. Oldham was at the forefront of this activity.

The town had ample supplies of coal (there were 37 local mines in 1832). These could power the steam engines on which the new cotton mills relied. There was a plentiful supply of water for those steam engines coming from the hills and moors above Oldham and there was a damp atmosphere necessary for cotton spinning. An influx of population from rural areas ensured there was a sufficient workforce. It helped that employers, like the Mellodews, built houses to accommodate them.

By 1855 Oldham had 96 cotton mills employing 11,400 people. Platt Brothers and Asa Lees were manufacturing textile machinery in the town and were to become known world wide. It was reckoned by Douglas Farnie in *The English Cotton Industry and the World Market* that in 1860 cotton manufacture accounted for 38.3 per cent of the value of domestic exports. Oldham led the way in satisfying such demand.

Its importance was recognised when the township of Oldham was incorporated by Royal Charter in 1849; this laid out the system of local government with the town becoming the Borough of Oldham. Similar recognition was achieved in parish terms with what was described as the parish of 'Prestwich cum Oldham' becoming 'Oldham cum Prestwich', and later still the parish of Oldham.

It is against this background that many cotton spinners set up in business, often at first by renting a few rooms in an existing mill building.

Given sufficient application, such was the demand for cotton yarn and cotton goods, that it was not difficult to make a good living as a Master Cotton Spinner. Such a rise in fortune is humorously described in Mr Bowker's *Lancashire Under the Hammer*, published in 1928.

But the phrase 'clogs to clogs in three generations' is well known. There will be few cotton families that cannot look back to clogs and an operative forebear inside three generations. The skill was to rise above the position of an operative and to hold on to the money then made.

Oldham had the capacity to produce cotton yarn and goods on a huge scale. Its downfall was the change in overseas markets, their ability to produce the goods themselves and Lancashire's inability to recognise what was happening and adapt competitively. In 1925 there were 59.9 million cotton spindles in the Lancashire cotton mills. By 1955 the figure was 29.2 million and by 1960 a mere 12 million.

The decline was mirrored in Oldham itself. Once a thriving industrial town with wealthy residents, by 1960 few of them were cotton mill proprietors and many had left the town. Within a decade a large number of its cotton mills had been demolished and those that remained, such as Vale Mill at Hollinwood, had been put to other uses.

Thus, Oldham today is very different from what it was. It has a Sainsbury's store, it has a sort of ring road, it has a tram to Manchester, it has a vibrant Art Gallery, it still has the Coliseum Theatre; it has a different ethnic population compared to earlier times. But it is clear that it struggles. Some of its former civic buildings were boarded up for years and are only now being brought to life. Some of its shops wear a 'hang-dog look'. It has lost its Stock Exchange, its mills, its wealth and, some would say, its soul as cotton is no longer in its blood and providing its vibrancy.

Family Trees

The Mannock Family

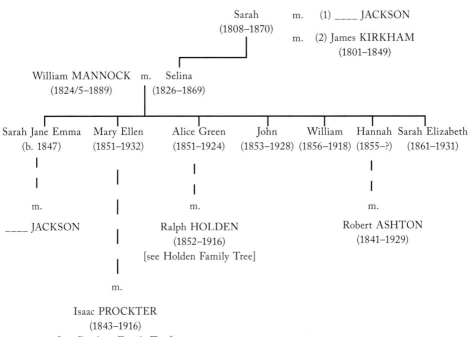

Sarah   m.   (1) ____ JACKSON
(1808–1870)

    m.   (2) James KIRKHAM
               (1801–1849)

William MANNOCK m. Selina
(1824/5–1889)   (1826–1869)

Sarah Jane Emma	Mary Ellen	Alice Green	John	William	Hannah	Sarah Elizabeth
(b. 1847)	(1851–1932)	(1851–1924)	(1853–1928)	(1856–1918)	(1855–?)	(1861–1931)

m.

____ JACKSON

m.

Ralph HOLDEN
(1852–1916)
[see Holden Family Tree]

m.

Robert ASHTON
(1841–1929)

m.

Isaac PROCKTER
(1843–1916)
[see Prockter Family Tree]

The Holden Family

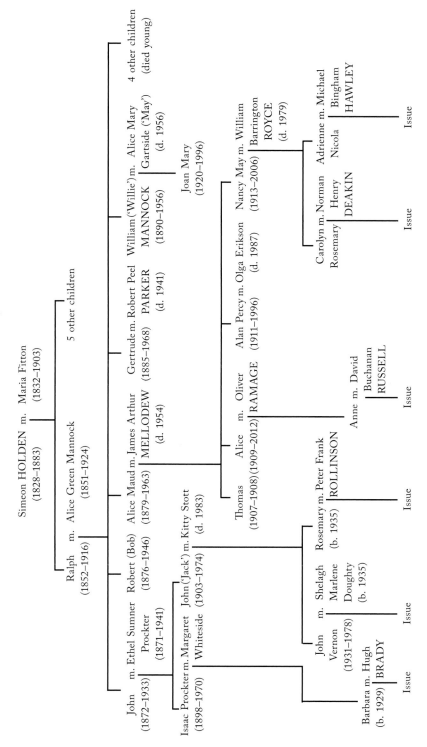

The Prockter Family

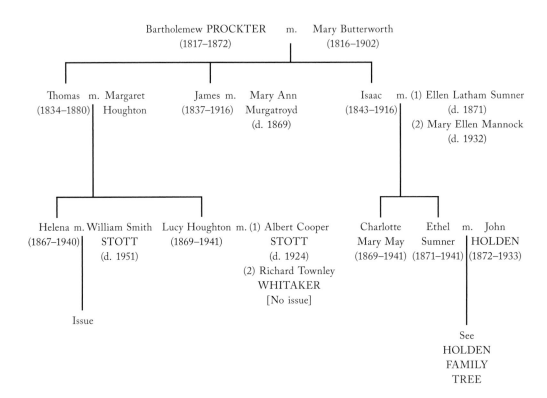

Bartholemew PROCKTER m. Mary Butterworth
(1817–1872) (1816–1902)

Thomas m. Margaret
(1834–1880) Houghton

James m. Mary Ann
(1837–1916) Murgatroyd
(d. 1869)

Isaac m. (1) Ellen Latham Sumner
(1843–1916) (d. 1871)
(2) Mary Ellen Mannock
(d. 1932)

Helena m. William Smith
(1867–1940) STOTT
(d. 1951)

Lucy Houghton m. (1) Albert Cooper
(1869–1941) STOTT
(d. 1924)
(2) Richard Townley
WHITAKER
[No issue]

Charlotte Ethel m. John
Mary May Sumner HOLDEN
(1869–1941) (1871–1941) (1872–1933)

Issue

See
HOLDEN
FAMILY
TREE

Cotton Terms

THE FIRMS OF KIRKHAM & MANNOCK Limited and Prockter & Co. Limited described themselves as 'Cotton Spinners and Doublers'. It might be helpful to the reader to have an idea what these, and other terms mentioned, mean (with apologies to those who already know!).

A cotton spinning firm ultimately produces the yarn which is used for weaving cloth, the weaving manufacturing everything from cotton velvet to underwear, from handkerchieves to sheets, from scarves to shirtings, from all types of indoor cotton clothing to outerwear; nowadays the cotton being often mixed with artificial fibres during the weaving process.

To arrive at the point where the yarn is actually formed, the raw cotton passes through a number of processes. It is not necessary to describe these here, other than to mention that the processes were sufficiently numerous to be very labour intensive. This explains why so many operatives were engaged in the Lancashire cotton spinning industry.

The spun cotton could be doubled, by the yarn being combined so as to produce a sewing thread, which would be stronger than ordinary yarn.

The yarn or thread so produced was then sold on, if not spun to order. It was a perceived defect of the Lancashire cotton industry that there was little vertical integration. It was not common for spinners to produce woven cloth with their own yarn, nor for weavers to engage in the dyeing of their manufactured cloth.

The Mellodews of Moorside, for instance, started out there as weavers of fustians and cotton velvets. They only undertook spinning so as to ensure a supply of cotton yarn of the consistency necessary for the weaving of the high quality velvets for which they became known. But the woven goods were sent out to independent dyers.

To turn now to various terms referred to in this book:

Cop: a tube carrying spun yarn.

Cotton Waste: bits of cotton yarn, later combined together to produce cleaning or wiping rags, deemed to be the most effective material for cleaning the grease and oil of railway locomotives for instance, useful in hospitals for absorbent pads, and probably used in the manufacture of book paper from 1790 until 1870.

Doubling: where two or more threads are compounded and twisted together for extra strength or smoothness, for instance to make sewing thread, lace and carpet thread, tent thread and thread for crocheting and hosiery.

Mule: a spinning machine created by Samuel Crompton in 1790 combining the elements of the spinning jenny, invented by James Hargreaves, and the water frame, invented by Richard Arkwright, and so named as it was a hybrid of these two machines. It was a rival to the Ring Frame.

Ring Frame: a spinning machine in which the spindle turns within a ring providing a continuous process where the roving was drawn, twisted and wrapped in one action.

Roving: a piece of cotton fibre drawn out and twisted preparatory to spinning.

Spindle: a thin tube on to which the spun yarn is wound. An average cotton mill in the 1890s would contain over 60 mules each with 1320 spindles (ie. 79,200 spindles)

List of Illustrations

Note on the value of money

T AKING A HISTORIC FIGURE of money and translating it into a modern day equivalent is almost impossible to do with any accuracy. Inflation has altered the value of money and the criteria for calculating inflation can be changed.

In my book *An Oldham Velvet Dynasty – the Mellodews of Moorside*, I used a table provided by the Office of National Statistics for the Retail Price Index from 1915 to give a modern day equivalent of sums mentioned in my text. On reflection, this index would appear to be conservative.

In his book *Splendour and Squalor* (Atlantic Books 2009 ISBN 978-1-84354-124-0) the journalist Marcus Scriven refers to a completely different method of calculation from that used by me. He says that 'the figures produced are much higher than those solely reliant on any inflation index', and avers that they are therefore more credible. That they are higher is shown by his figure of someone leaving an estate of £25,000 in March 1916, which he says is the equivalent of £8.69 million in 2009; my method of calculation would have produced a comparative figure of £1.1 million.

However, even Mr Scriven concedes that his method of calculation can give rise to inaccuracy. He quotes from James Lees-Milne's diary entry for 9 June 1991 in which Lees-Milne recorded an assertion by Roy Jenkins, a former Chancellor of the Exchequer, that the money of 1941 could be converted to that of 1991 by multiplying by 40. Lees-Milne replied that a great-aunt of his had been living at No. 5 Royal Crescent, Bath, with a cook, a parlour maid and a housemaid, on £600 per annum. Jenkins conceded that no one would 'get far on £24,000' (ie. £600 x 40) in 1991.

This anecdote, like house prices, is to favour higher figures and is therefore of more dramatic effect. During this period, as one knows from one's own experience, other costs, such as telephone costs and the price of electrical appliances, have come down. The composition of any Index used will of course change as some items comprised in the original index will be replaced in the index by other items (such as electrical goods) which were not around at the inception of the Index.

In short, any comparison is a rough figure. I have in mind that inflation splits itself into periods as under:

- 1715–1914: 92% (a period of 200 years averaging 0.33% pa inflation)

- 1914–18: 103% (First World War)

- 1918–39: minus 13% (depression)

- 1939–45: 51% (Second World War)

- 1945–70: 179%

- 1970–82: 338% (supply shocks, oil etc.)

As it appears to me that Mr Scriven's basis of calculation is too generous, and my previous calculation too much the other way, I have taken a very rough and ready figure of comparison which treats one pound in 1918 as worth around £40 today, whilst one pound in 1914 or earlier is worth about £80 today, with the appropriate percentages for the years between these two dates.

For periods between 1918 and 1939, I have used a multiplier of 40 and thereafter I have reverted to the Office of National Statistics Retail Price Index figures plus 50 per cent. In view of the conjecture about such calculations (see for instance the Table of Prices published in *The Economist* on 13 July 1974 showing a table of prices going back to 1661) this very rough and ready calculation seems as good as any!

I have not translated every figure mentioned in the text into a possible modern day equivalent as that might prove tedious to the reader, concerning myself instead with only those figures which are worthy of emphasis.

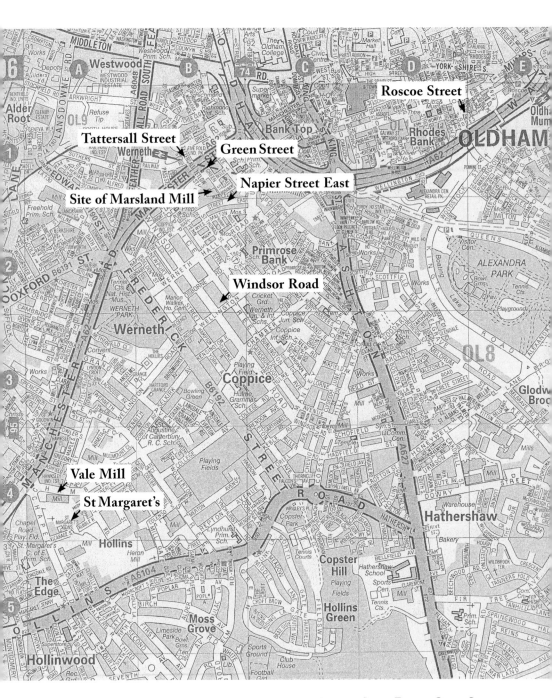

1. Map of Oldham (2007) showing proximity of Napier Street East to Green Street (the site of Marsland Mills), St Margaret's, Hollinwood to Vale Mill, Bank Top, Roscoe Street, Mumps and Windsor Road (Courtesy of Greater Manchester A–Z Geographers' A–Z Map Co. Ltd)

CHAPTER ONE

The Founding of Kirkham & Mannock: Mr William Mannock (1825–89)

WHEN SARAH JACKSON MARRIED James Kirkham she already had two children, Selina (born 1826 when Sarah was only 17) and James Stanley Jackson (born 1831).

By the time of the 1841 Census, Mr and Mrs Kirkham and her two Jackson children were listed as living at Bent, Lower, Oldham Below Town. Mr Kirkham was described as a Draper. All of his neighbours appear to have been hatters, an occupation fast being replaced by employment in the expanding cotton mills. Mr Kirkham was some seven years older than his wife, having been born in 1801.

The same census lists the household of Thomas Mannock (spelt Manocks in the Census), consisting of his wife Betty and six children, including the eldest son, William, born in 1825. Mr Thomas Mannock was described as a hatter.

Both families are shown with the same address, although in different dwellings. It is not perhaps surprising therefore that William Mannock should marry Selina Jackson. The wedding took place at St Mary's Church, Prestwich, in 1845 when Selina was 19 and her groom aged 21. Their first child, Sarah Jane Emma Mannock (known as Emma), was born in 1847.

Mr Kirkham died in 1849 and one has to assume that his occupation had allowed him 'to put a little by', which went to his widow.

By the time of the 1851 Census, the widowed Mrs Kirkham, still only 43, had set herself up as a Beerseller. She was described as head of household at York Street, Oldham.

This was a full household consisting of Mrs Kirkham, her son James (shown as a Blacksmith), her daughter Selina and son-in-law William Mannock and

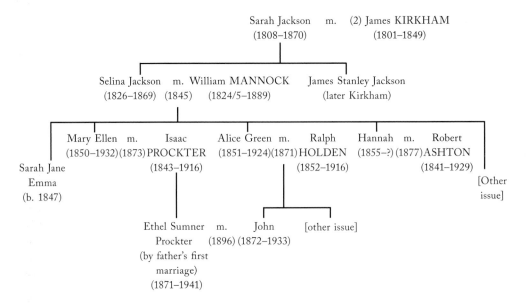

2. Family Tree (extract) showing Mannock, Holden and Prockter families

their three children, Emma, Mary Ellen and Alice Green Mannock. Hannah Mannock (William's young sister aged 15, a cotton weaver), Emma Kerfoot, and her infant son James, aged one month, completed the list of occupants. With a household of ten, including four children, it was not surprising that the occupations of Selina Mannock and Emma Kerfoot were described as 'domestic duties'!

This 1851 Census describes William Mannock as a Cotton Waste Dealer, aged 26. Nothing is known about his early business activities, but it would seem that the firm of Kirkham & Mannock would have been established in the decade prior to 1861, for Slater's 1861 *Directory of Oldham* lists the firm of Kirkham & Mannock as 'Cotton Spinners and Doublers' at Lyon Mill, Tattersall Street, Werneth, Oldham.

That Census describes Mrs Kirkham as a cotton spinner employing 85 hands. William Mannock's occupation is also shown as a cotton spinner. Whether or not he was still trading as a cotton waste dealer is not known.

As Douglas Farnie has pointed out, it was not unusual for a fledgling business to rent power and space in another's building. This reduced the amount of capital required to begin a business and if business went well, further space could be taken in the building.

Duncan Gurr's excellent book, *The Cotton Mills of Oldham*, tells us that

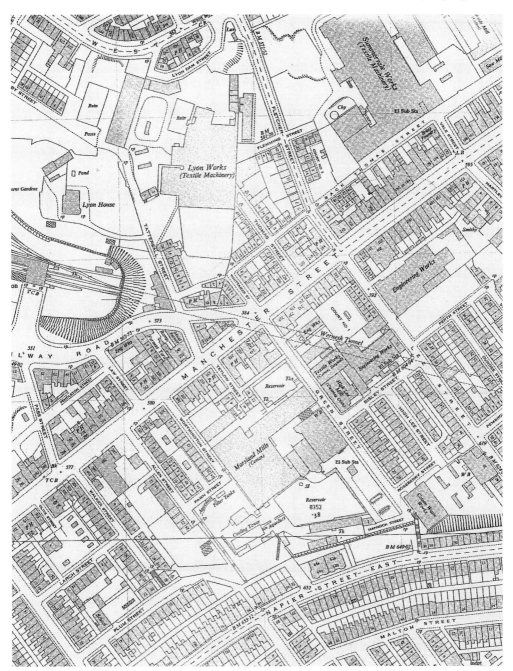

3. 1955 Map showing the position of the Marsland Mills, Green Street and nearby
Napier Street East, Oldham and showing the extent of Marsland Mills (courtesy
Oldham Local Studies and Archives)

4. Marsland Mills *c.*1970 (shown top left) at the time of redevelopment of land in the foreground also showing (top left corner) part of 62/64 Napier Street East (courtesy Oldham Local Studies and Archives)

Lyon Mill was an old building constructed by John Tattersall between 1821 and 1824. Mr Tattersall was a cotton spinner also making fustians and shirting employing, by 1861, some 430 hands. The building would therefore have been of a reasonable size but with surplus space which could be rented out.

By 1861 Mrs Kirkham, Mr and Mrs Mannock, and their eight children were residing at Tattersall Street, hard by the Lyon Mill.

Further business space was taken at Marsland Mill, in nearby Green Street. This again was an old building built in 1827. It was at one time occupied by Mayall and Wild employing 200 hands, so was not a huge building. Kirkham & Mannock were to consolidate their business on this site.

The exact business arrangement between Mrs Kirkham and William Mannock is not known but when she died on 25 February 1870 a Dissolution of Partnership Notice was inserted in the *London Gazette*, usual for the time, announcing the dissolution of the partnership between the late Mrs Kirkham, William Mannock and Stanley Jackson trading as Kirkham, Mannock and

Jackson. Interestingly the firm is described as 'Cotton Spinners' carrying on business at Marsland Mill, Lyon Mill and Summervale Mill.

The Summervale Mill was situate in Fletcher Street, Oldham, near to Tattersall Street and Green Street. Duncan Gurr describes it as tenanted by a number of different concerns of which, doubtless, Kirkham & Mannock was one.

The death of Selina Mannock, William's wife, in 1869, aged 43, from arthritis, and the death of his mother in law the following year must have allowed William Mannock to consolidate his interests. What happened to the interest of Stanley Jackson is not known but by 2 April 1871 (the date of the 1871 Census) William Mannock had moved his family from Tattersall Street to Green Street, adjacent to Marsland Mill.

And in the same year, whilst still occupying the original Marsland Mill, he erected the No. 2 Mill. This was a substantial property for Mr Mannock is described in the Census as employing 242 hands (of whom 85 were males). This is an almost threefold increase on the figure ten years earlier.

Mr Mannock called his house in Green Street 'Marsland House' which suggests a larger abode than his neighbours. It was obviously sensible to live close to the business so that it could be properly directed and supervised.

It is noteworthy that the Mannocks, and later the Holdens for two generations, always lived within easy walking distance of their mill premises. This was common at the time. The exodus from Oldham to South Manchester, the Fylde Coast and the Lake District by mill owners had not yet begun.

Mr Mannock being now a widower, and his eldest daughter Emma having left home on her marriage, house was kept for him by his daughters Mary Ellen and Alice Green Mannock, aged 20 and 22 respectively, assisted by one domestic servant respectably aged 47, the same age as her master.

These two daughters were to make marriages of significance so far as this short history is concerned. Alice was to marry Ralph Holden in 1871 and Mary Ellen was to marry Isaac Prockter in 1873; Ethel Sumner Prockter, a daughter by Isaac's first marriage, was later to marry a son of Ralph and Alice Holden, thus helping to combine the respective business interests of these three families – Mannocks, Holdens and Prockters.

The late 1860s and 1870s was a time of great expansion in the cotton industry. The American Civil War, with its cotton famine and hardship for Lancashire, was past and the number of spindles in Oldham doubled in the five years to 1871. By that year, as Farnie reports, Oldham had more spindles than any country in the world outside the USA; it maintained that position of superiority until 1937.

The years 1873 to 1875 were reported to have seen a great building boom. This was the time of the 'Oldham Limiteds'; new limited liability companies were incorporated which raised capital locally, usually by the issue of partly paid shares, and by accepting loans on which interest was paid. New mills were built with the monies raised. The banking system as we know it was not fully established and banks were subject to failure (for instance, Fenton's Bank in Rochdale); it was attractive to the local inhabitants to invest in companies whose buildings they could see and whose business appeared to be booming.

Although the No. 2 Marsland Mill was built during this period, there is no evidence that Kirkham & Mannock took outside loans, and it was not to be an incorporated company until later (see Chapter Four). Mr Mannock presumably financed the expansion of his trade by remaining in modest domestic accommodation and ploughing his profits back in to the business.

Oldham spinning continued to boom, and Kirkham & Mannock's No. 2 Mill was extended in 1880.

Illustration No 3 shows the extent of the mills in 1955, and it will be seen that Green Street runs alongside, the Marsland Mills.

The 1881 Census shows William Mannock still living at Marsland House, 18 Green Street, the housekeeping having devolved upon his youngest daughter Sarah Elizabeth (known as Sarah) (then aged 20) assisted by one servant. At the time of the Census, daughter Mary Ellen Prockter was staying, no doubt keeping an eye on her sister's housekeeping, but also keeping an eye on building works at 62 and 64 (together known as 'West Bank') Napier Street East, Oldham.

Oldham cotton spinners' prosperity meant that Mr Mannock, like many others, could afford to upgrade his living arrangements. By 1884 he and his daughter were living at No. 64 Napier Street East whilst his daughter Mary Ellen, married to Isaac Prockter, was living next door at 62.

This did not mean that Mr Mannock moved away from his mills! It will be seen from the map that Napier Street East is adjacent to the Marsland Mills. What the map does not show is that Napier Street East stands well above the mills. Even today there are steep steps down from Napier Street East to Green Street. Mr Mannock was thus not far from his empire.

Nor was he far from his family for he had one daughter living with him, another next door and his daughter Alice and her husband, Ralph Holden, with their family, now moved into Marsland House.

The picture of Marsland Mills taken at the time of redevelopment of the surrounding area in about 1970, shows the old No. 1 Mill very much dwarfed by the later No. 2 Mill to its right (both top left in the picture). The picture also shows part of 62/64 Napier Street East standing high above the mills (acute top left).

With such expansion of business, it is unlikely that Mr Mannock had much time to be involved in civic affairs, and so little is known about him. But, like so many in Oldham at that time, he would have been conscious of its civic pride in becoming an important industrial town. He contributed to its first exhibition of local industry in December 1885 by presenting a cop spun in his own mills and a much earlier cop spun in 1735 acquired by him, having been found in Manchester in 1882.

William Mannock died at 14, The Promenade, Southport on 16 June 1889, aged 65. His son-in-law Isaac Prockter registered the death. At the time of Mr Mannock's death another expansion of the Marsland Mills was planned to take place. This, combined with the earlier extension of 1880, suggests a considerable expansion of business. This accords with a general mill-building splurge in Oldham.

This mini-boom, so Farnie tells us, raised the average size of the spinning mill from 50,000 spindles in 1873/5 to 75,000 spindles in 1889/90. Kirkham & Mannock followed this norm.

5. Exhibition Frame showing cop spun at Marsland Mills *c*.1885
(courtesy Gallery Oldham)

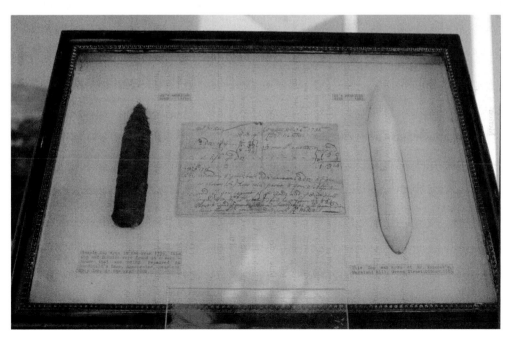

Grace's Guide to British Industrial History shows that Kirkham & Mannock had 80,000 spindles in 1891. By contrast Isaac Seville & Sons at Coppice Mill, Waterhead, Oldham had only 3,200 spindles and William H. Smith at Austerlands Mill 2,400 spindles. The much longer established Thomas Mellodew & Co. at Moorside, Oldham, had 80,000 spindles whilst Thomas Emmott & Sons Limited had 84,700 spindles. In terms of size, therefore, Kirkham & Mannock were towards the top tier of Oldham cotton spinners.

So, the draper's capital inherited by Mrs Kirkham and the undoubted energy and entrepreneurial spirit of her son-in-law William Mannock founded the firm of Kirkham & Mannock. Profits were ploughed back and the Marsland Mills expanded. The interest of William Mannock's own sons-in-law Ralph Holden and Isaac Prockter no doubt helped to stoke the success of the firm. All lived within close proximity. All three men had an interest in its prosperity, the sons-in-law for obvious reasons!

It is appropriate therefore that we should look at each of these two men in turn before we turn to the complications of William Mannock's Will.

CHAPTER TWO

Ralph Holden (1852–1916): an energetic man of business

RALPH HOLDEN WAS BORN in Royton, near Oldham, in 1852. He soon made his mark on the business and commercial world of Oldham. Besides his interest, inherited from his father Simeon Holden (1828–83), in the firm of Simeon Holden (later Simeon Holden Limited), cotton and cotton waste dealers, he was a director of Bank Top Spinning Co. from the youthful age of 22 years. He was both a shareholder and provider of working capital by way of loan to that firm, which was situate very close to the centre of Oldham.

How he came to be connected to Bank Top at such an early age, one does not know. It would appear that his directorship of Bank Top Spinning Co. came after a rebuilding of that mill following fires in 1872 and 1874. His business as a cotton waste dealer would bring him into contact with many Oldham mill owners, and his flair for business and energy would have been an attraction.

The business of Simeon Holden was carried out at 6 and 8 Roscoe Street, very close to Mumps Bridge, a well known Oldham landmark. His main business interests would not therefore be more than a mile apart (see Illustration 1).

Simeon Holden had married his wife Maria on 23 September 1849, when he was just 21. Ralph also made an early marriage. This marriage in late 1871 to William Mannock's third child Alice Green Mannock brought advantage as her father's cotton spinning business, Kirkham & Mannock, was not insignificant, employing nearly 250 workers. It will be recalled that William Mannock had also started his business life as a cotton waste dealer.

By 1881 Mr and Mrs Ralph Holden, both now in their early 30s, were living at 6 Herbert Street, Waterhead, Oldham. This was a respectable enough address off the Ripponden Road, leading up to Moorside and thence to Halifax. The district of Waterhead had been home to Simeon Holden for many years. However it was an inconvenient distance from the Marsland Mills.

Following the death of Simeon Holden in 1883, it is not surprising that by 1884 the Holdens had moved into Marsland House, 18 Green Street, Oldham when Mr Mannock moved to Napier Street East.

By residing in Green Street, Oldham, it was inevitable that Ralph Holden should be drawn into the affairs of Kirkham & Mannock and indeed was probably invited to do so as his father in law approached the age of 60.

Whilst Mr Mannock had sons, neither John Mannock nor William Mannock (Junior) was disposed to join their father in business and by the time of William Mannock's death in 1889 it is probable that Ralph Holden was the driving force behind Kirkham & Mannock, responsible for the building expansion of 1880 and 1890. Worrall's Directory for the time suggests that he still had his other interests as he is described both as a 'Cotton Spinner' and a 'Cotton Waste Dealer.'

As we have seen, by 1891 Kirkham & Mannock were listed as having 80,000 spindles. It probably suited them to remain at this size. It lessened the risk. It also suited them to remain as cotton spinners and doublers rather than extend themselves by branching into weaving or other more risky activities.

By 1891 they had a telegraphic address – 'Lion. Oldham' – and by 1895 were a member of Manchester's Royal Exchange, with a position at Pillar No. 12. The Royal Exchange in Manchester had been established in 1804 and has been described as 'the pivot of Manchester's central business district'. It was the place to meet the influential merchants who sold raw cotton and who purchased the spun yarn. To be a member was to show that one's business 'had arrived'.

The Mellodews at Moorside were slightly ahead of Kirkham & Mannock having been members of the Royal Exchange since 1852 and being connected to the telephone!

Ralph Holden obviously prospered, for he acquired a large range of interests as diverse geographically as Globe Spinning Co., Macclesfield and J. & J. Rigby in Salford, in addition to his interests in Kirkham & Mannock, Simeon Holden and Bank Top Spinning.

Domestically, the household at 18, Green Street, would have been busy. There were nine children, of whom five survived, namely John, Robert, Alice Maud, Gertrude and William Mannock Holden. Frank, William, Ralph (Junior) and Gerald Holden all died under the age of 21 years unmarried and without children. A family of such size, and deaths in infancy, was not unusual for Victorian times. As Pat Jalland, writing in *Women, Marriage and Politics 1860–1914*, says, 'Between 1860 and 1900 over 14% of infants in England and Wales died before their first birthday'.

6. Mr Ralph Holden

Shortly after William Mannock's death in 1889, Ralph Holden and his family moved from Green Street to William Mannock's former home at West Bank, 64, Napier Street East. Thus, Mrs Holden was to live next door to her sister Mary Ellen Prockter at No. 62.

'Aunt Sarah', who had been looking after her father, moved to 61, Belgrave Road, Oldham, respectably near Alexandra Park, but not being quite so fashionable an area as the Coppice district of Oldham. Moving with her was Helen Hamner, who by 1901 had been with her 40 year old mistress for over 20 years.

It must have been with great satisfaction that Ralph Holden saw the marriage of his eldest son John to Ethel Sumner Prockter, Isaac Prockter's second daughter, at St Thomas's Church, Werneth, Oldham on 8 July 1896. While this was a marriage to 'the girl next door', it brought the Holden and Prockter interests closer together. Ralph Holden and Isaac Prockter had both married Mannock girls. Isaac only had two children by his earlier marriage and Ethel's elder sister, May Prockter, did not seem as if she would marry. In course therefore, it was likely that Isaac's wealth would devolve upon Ethel and any children she might have. Satisfactory indeed!

A man like Ralph Holden does not stand still and contacts are all important. This probably explains his entrance into local politics, his membership of the

Oldham Master Cotton Spinners Association and Federation of Lancashire Cotton Spinners and being a committee member of both those organisations. He was also a Freemason, another source of contacts.

So far as politics are concerned, Ralph Holden was a Liberal, being elected to Oldham Borough Council as representative for Mumps Ward in 1905.

This was a time when the Labour Party was in its infancy, candidates first standing for election in 1892 and there not being a Labour Prime Minister until Ramsay Macdonald in 1924. Meantime, political power oscillated between the Conservative Party of Disraeli, Lord Salisbury and then Arthur Balfour (Prime Minister 1902–05) and the Liberal Party of Gladstone, Lord Rosebery and Herbert Campbell-Bannerman (Prime Minister 1905–08).

Although Winston Churchill was elected Conservative MP for Oldham in 1900 when the Conservative party held sway under the Marquess of Salisbury (before joining the Liberal party in 1904), in general the Oldham businessmen favoured the Liberal party, as they believed in free trade. Typical of their views might be those of Thomas Mellodew, the velvet manufacturer of Moorside, Oldham, who some years earlier when asked for his political views was able to point to a bust of Richard Cobden (1804–65) in the corner of his office and say 'those, sir, are my politics'. Cobden was of course the great advocate of free trade, had advocated the repeal of the Corn Laws, and latterly was the MP for nearby Rochdale.

It was a volatile time in politics. Ralph Holden was elected to Oldham Borough Council after defeating the sitting Councillor Dixon by 22 votes. After his three years' service, Councillor Dixon regained the seat by 82 votes. Never one to accept defeat, Ralph Holden stood again in 1911 and was elected by 46 votes. Close contests were obviously a feature of Oldham Council elections (see post p. 17). He finally retired from politics in 1913.

During the time he was on the Council, he was a member of the important Watch Committee and the Carrying and Cleansing Committee (originally known as the Horses and Provender Committee). His obituary in the *Oldham Chronicle* reports that as a member of the latter committee, and Chairman from 1912, he instigated a thorough reorganisation to improve its efficiency. This accords with what is known about his business interests – solid progressive growth at Kirkham & Mannock accompanied by a building up of personal assets accumulated through a modest and prudent lifestyle, everything orderly and methodical but pursued with energy.

CHAPTER THREE

Mr Isaac Prockter (1843–1916): a solid man of business

THE PROCKTERS ARE INTEGRAL to this history because they linked the Mannock and Holden families. They also provided the link to the important Stott family that we shall come to later.

Before we look at Isaac Prockter, we must first look at his father, Bartholomew.

Bartholomew was a Yorkshireman, being born outside Halifax in 1817. In the 1841 Census he described himself as a Farmer, and was living at Dearnley about two miles north east of Rochdale and no more than ten miles from Oldham. His wife Mary, who was one year his senior, came from Rochdale. They were married at St Leonard's Church, Middleton in July 1834, when they were both 17.

Farming in those days would have been on a subsistence level, and soon with four youngsters to provide for (Mary Ann, James, Thomas and John) Bartholomew must have taken the decision to join the cotton industry. Such a change of occupation was not unusual at the time as it provided more opportunity for advancement.

Bartholomew Prockter's decision mirrored that of James Mellodew (1816–83) who abandoned his father's cabbage patch in 1832 to join his brothers in the cotton trade, and helped to found Thomas Mellodew & Co. at Moorside, Oldham. The *Oldham Chronicle* in July 1882 graphically described young Mellodew's position:

> The scene is Castleton Moor, a place from which the few chimneys which then marked the site of Oldham could be seen. In a field hoeing potatoes stands a boy of about thirteen years of age. From time to time he ceases from his work and, leaning on his hoe, looks longingly in the direction of Oldham.

7. St Leonard's
   Church,
   Middleton

He is thinking of the bleakness of his future if he continues to labour in the fields. Why should he not go out as his brothers before him have done and seek a livelihood in the cotton trade? He pricks the tool straight upwards in the ground and over hedge and ditch makes his way to what appears to him to be the promised land.

Mr Prockter must have done well for by 1861 Bartholomew could describe himself as a cotton spinner. About that time he allied himself with Nathaniel Littler from Ashton-in-Makerfield, near Wigan. Mr Littler, a draper, was 11 years older than Bartholomew and how they became connected is a bit of a mystery. It is possible that he provided the capital for their joint venture.

8. Bartholomew Prockter

Vale Mill, adjacent to Chamber Road, Hollinwood, was built in 1868 and Worrall's Directory for 1871 lists both Bartholomew Prockter and Isaac Prockter as cotton spinners trading there as Prockter, Littler & Co. and employing 250 hands (about the same as Kirkham & Mannock).

This area of Hollinwood is about one and a half miles south of Oldham town centre, towards Manchester.

Mr Littler moved from Ashton-in-Makerfield to live near the mill. By 1881 he described himself as a 'retired Cotton Spinner'. He was then 75! The firm became Prockter & Co. Ltd. Ownership was proudly embellished on the façade.

Meantime, Isaac Prockter (Bartholomew's fifth child, born in 1843) had married Ellen Latham Sumner on 5 August 1868 at St Thomas's Church, Ashton-in-Makerfield. His bride was 24 (born 2 March 1844) the daughter of John Sumner, an Iron Merchant.

Unfortunately, whilst Isaac's marriage produced two children, Charlotte Mary May Prockter (always known as 'May') and Ethel Sumner Prockter, it was short lived. Their mother died on 2 May 1871 when the two little girls were aged one and a few months respectively. A service was held at St Margaret's Church, Hollinwood.

9. Vale Mill frontage to Chamber Road, Oldham

10. Façade inscription on Vale Mill (2016)

The proximity of Vale Mill to St Margaret's Church can be seen from the map (Illustration 11 – although of a later period than 1871). Isaac was then living at 312 Manchester Road, Oldham (just off the top left hand corner of the map) and so was within easy walking distance of the mill and the Church. His father was living at Hardcroft, Middleton Road, Chadderton, Oldham, a comfortable walking distance from the mill.

Bartholomew Prockter died in the June quarter of 1872, aged 55, leaving the firm in the hands of Isaac and his brother Thomas.

Shortly afterwards Isaac Prockter married again, this time to Mary Ellen Mannock, one of William Mannock's daughters. The marriage took place at St Margaret's on 30 April 1873. William Mannock, his daughter Hannah, who was later to marry Robert Ashton (and of whom we shall hear later), and Isaac's brother, Thomas Prockter, were the witnesses.

For a moment we shall mention a little about Thomas, some nine years older than Isaac. He had four daughters of whom two, Helena and Lucy Houghton Prockter, were to marry into the important family of James Stott, also a cotton spinner and a very successful one. Further mention of the Stott family follows in Chapter Eleven.

The middle brother, James, whilst no doubt having an interest in Prockter & Co., was engaged in running the business of Buckley & Prockter, the large Oldham department store dominating the Oldham area of Mumps. He lived above the store. In 1861 he was described as an Assistant Draper to Mr Abraham Buckley. Mr Buckley had an interest in a Prockter enterprise with Bartholomew Prockter and Nathaniel Littler, which was dissolved in 1867. It is suggested that a judicious marriage in 1863 between James Prockter and Mr Buckley's niece, Mary Ann Murgatroyd, resulted in the subsequent firm of Buckley and Prockter. The couple had two children who both died at birth with James's wife dying in 1869. Buckley & Prockter were regarded as the leading Oldham store. They described themselves as 'House Furnishers, Funeral Directors, Ladies Outfitters, Costumiers and Milliners, Men's and Boy's Outfitters and Tailors and General Drapers'.

12. Mr Isaac Prockter

James was clearly well known in the town, sitting as a Liberal Councillor for St James's ward from 1 November 1886, taking his seat from his Conservative opponent by just four votes, being one of the 'great and the good' who attended the Mayoral luncheon at Oldham Town Hall on 17 June 1889 to celebrate the jubilee of the incorporation of the Borough of Oldham, and becoming a JP in 1893.

The store enjoyed considerable expansion as is illustrated by a bill heading of 1941. As this book is not about Buckley & Prockter, one will merely note that the store having been extended in 1897, it was demolished to make way for a roundabout in 1966. The store is remembered in Helen Bradley's book *Miss Carter came with us*, set supposedly in 1908 and mis-spelling the Prockter name.

BOUGHT OF

BUCKLEY & PROCKTER LTD.

MUMPS

OLDHAM

PHONE:
MAIN 3481
(3 LINES)

MEN'S & BOYS
OUTFITTERS
AND TAILORS

HOUSE FURNISHERS
FUNERAL DIRECTORS
LADIES' OUTFITTERS
COSTUMIERS & MILLINERS

H.2. GENERAL DRAPERS

Exors of:
Mrs. Holden, "Brentwood"   20th Sept. 1941.

186, Windsor Road, OLDHAM.

			10	11	
July 11	1 Hose				
		1	15	6	
" 18	Black Felt Hat				
		1	0	0	
" 19	" " "				
		4	19	6	
Aug. 1	Chauffer's Raincoat				
		2	5	6	
" 1	Pink Blouse				
		8	8	0	
Sept. 6	Evening Coat				
			16	11	
" 6	Gloves				
		9	16	0	
" 8	Black Coat				
		29	12	4	
July 17	By return of Black				
	Hat	1. 0. 0			
Aug. 4	By return of Black				
	Cardigan Suit.	11.11. 0	12	11	0
			17	1	4
			1	14	1
	Less 10% discount.		15	7	3

13. 1941 Bill Heading of Buckley & Prockter Limited showing the store's façades

14. The Mumps (Oldham) store of Buckley & Procter (incorrectly spelt) as illustrated in Helen Bradley's *Miss Carter came with us*, set in 1908

Thomas Prockter died in 1880 so that the running of Prockter & Co. devolved to Isaac alone.

By 1884, Isaac Prockter and his second wife Mary Ellen (née Mannock) and unmarried daughters, May and Ethel Sumner Prockter, were living at 62, Napier Street East, next door to Mary's sister Sarah Elizabeth and their father William Mannock. Sometime after his death in 1889 the adjoining No. 64 was taken on by Ralph Holden and his wife Alice. The two sisters were therefore living next door to each other.

This was apparently very convenient for small children, who taken on a visit, did not want to go home. There was a large attic which ran across both houses with no dividing wall. A granddaughter (Alice Ramage, née Mellodew) recalls being able to go up the staircase of one house and down the staircase of the other – the perfect escape!

By the end of the nineteenth century the Prockters were a solidly established family; Mrs Mary Prockter (Isaac's widowed mother) continued to live in a comfortable home on Middleton Road, Chadderton, Oldham, and could describe herself as 'an annuitant' in the 1881 Census, suggesting that she was receiving the equivalent of a pension from Prockter & Co. She died on 16 March 1902 leaving a respectable estate of £7,022 equally between her

15. Numbers 62 and 64 Napier Street East, Oldham (2010) later the Highpoint Hotel
(closed 2009)

six surviving children (including James and Isaac) with a further share going
to the children of Thomas, as he had died.

James was obviously well known and a solid citizen, a former councillor, JP
and the proprietor of Buckley & Prockter. Isaac was running Prockter & Co.
Limited at the prominent Vale Mill at Hollinwood. In 1891 the company was
listed as having 78,000 spindles, about the same as Kirkham & Mannock. Its
telegraphic address was 'Prockters. Hollinwood'. The Prockters could therefore
regard themselves as a prominent Oldham family.

We shall come to Isaac's more particular interest later, in Chapter Six.

CHAPTER FOUR

The complications of Mr William Mannock's Will

A T THE TIME OF HIS DEATH on 16 June 1889, William Mannock owned the cotton spinning business of Kirkham & Mannock. He was anxious to be fair to his seven surviving children. His will dated 11 August 1886, in effect, left his estate divided into seven equal parts. The executors were his sons-in-law Isaac Prockter (married to his daughter Mary Ellen) and Ralph Holden (married to his daughter Alice Green) and an outsider, Arthur Watts Newton.

The will was not however without complication. Firstly, he left income only from the respective one seventh shares to his children (the capital going to their children on their respective deaths). And, for reasons unknown, he limited the income that his married daughter Sarah Jane Emma Jackson could receive to 40 shillings per week, possibly because he disapproved of her husband? Secondly, he provided detailed provisions in relation to his son, John Mannock.

John, William's eldest son, had left the shores of England in or about 1878 and by 1886 had not been heard of since. His father therefore provided that in the event that John should not return or be heard of within two years following his death, then the one seventh share from which John was to receive income during his lifetime was to go in augmentation of the remaining six shares.

There is obviously speculation as to what prompted the disappearance of John Mannock. Did he violently disagree with his father? Did he in some way disgrace himself? In any event John did turn up as is evidenced by his mention in later court proceedings and the 1901 Census which shows him living with his wife Elizabeth, and her two children, at Parkfield Road, Failsworth, aged 49, and 'living on his own means'.

The will further provided that the executors and trustees could carry on the deceased's business. Whilst Ralph Holden was probably doing this already, with some involvement from his brother in law Isaac Prockter, this was an unsatisfactory state of affairs. As trustees, they would be conscious of the seven shares of the estate for which they were expected to provide income. Furthermore, should any of William Mannock's children die, their respective one seventh share passed down to their own children. In time therefore there would be a lot of disparate interests in the firm.

With this in mind, proposals were made to crystallise the value of the various one sevenths and to pay them out. However, as there were potential infant beneficiaries (the issue of William Mannock's children who were to get the capital on the death of their own parent) it was necessary to make application to the courts to get consent to the proposals. And so started a series of actions (albeit friendly) in the Chancery Palatine Court, based in Manchester.

By a series of orders of the court dated 10 April 1891, 1 August 1893 and 9 November 1896, it was established that the value of William Mannock's business as at 31 December 1890 was £57,591, so that a one seventh share was equal to £8,227. This was a considerable estate, equivalent to about £4,607,280 today, so that a one seventh share was worth £658,182, certainly making it possible for John Mannock to live 'on his own means'!

Consent was given to setting aside separate amounts of this sum to satisfy the interests of Emma Jackson (and her children) and Sarah Elizabeth Mannock (and her children, if any). Why the eldest and youngest children were dealt with first is not known. Possibly it was felt that they had the greatest need? After all, Sarah was unmarried and probably had few other means.

The order of 1893 made similar provision to satisfy the interest of John Mannock whilst the order of 1896 made a similar provision for William Mannock (Junior). Finally, by 1912 the court ordered £8,227 to be set aside to satisfy the interest of Mary Ellen Prockter (née Mannock).

In the years following William Mannock's death, although there were 'ups and downs', a recurring feature of the cotton trade, there was general prosperity amongst the mills of Oldham, with a boom in the years 1904–08.

The amounts needed to pay out the Mannock children were presumably found by cash generated by the deceased's business, borrowings and by the issue of shares once the business became incorporated.

By the time of the final order of 1912, the business of Kirkham & Mannock was controlled by Isaac Prockter and Ralph Holden as trustees and held for the interests of Alice Green Holden (Ralph's wife) and Hannah

1912.—Letter M.—No. 22.

In the Chancery of the

County Palatine of Lancaster.

MANCHESTER DISTRICT.

Folios 51.

IN THE MATTER of the ESTATE of WILLIAM MANNOCK deceased.

Between—

MARY ELLEN PROCKTER (Married Woman) - - - - - - *Plaintiff*

— AND —

ISAAC PROCKTER, RALPH HOLDEN and ALICE GREEN HOLDEN (his Wife), HANNAH ASHTON (Married Woman), JOHN HOLDEN, ROBERT HOLDEN, ALICE MAUD MELLODEW (Married Woman), GERTRUDE PARKER (Married Woman), WILLIAM MANNOCK HOLDEN, ADA MARY MILL (Married Woman), ROBERT ASHTON, ARTHUR WILLIAM ASHTON, SELINA MELDRUM (Married Woman), HAROLD ASHTON, DOROTHY MAY ASHTON (Spinster and Infant), and ARTHUR WATTS NEWTON, *Arthur Slater* *Sarah Elizabeth Mannock (Spinster) Henry Bootly Backhouse and William Ewing Ingham)* *Defendants.*

9th February, 1912.
All parties concerned in the matter of this Petition are to attend the Sittings of the Court to be holden at the Assize Courts, Manchester, on Monday, the 11th day of March, 1912, at 10.30 o'clock in the forenoon.

HUBERT WINSTANLEY,
Registrar.

To THE RIGHT HONOURABLE THE CHANCELLOR OF THE DUCHY AND COUNTY PALATINE OF LANCASTER.

THE HUMBLE PETITION of MARY ELLEN PROCKTER, the Wife of the Defendant, Isaac Prockter, of Napier Street, East Oldham, in the County of Lancaster.

SHEWETH as follows:—

1. The above-named deceased William Mannock late of Napier Street East aforesaid, Cotton Spinner, by his last Will bearing date the 11th day of August 1886 appointed his sons-in-law

16. 1912 Final court proceedings in William Mannock's estate
(front page of Summons)

Ashton, the two remaining children of William Mannock whose interests had not been paid out.

Hannah had married Robert Ashton at St Thomas's Church, Werneth, Oldham in mid-1877, when she was 22 and her husband was 36 years old. A farmer from Newton by Frodsham, Cheshire, where he had been born, and farming 120 acres and employing three labourers and two boys, he made up for lost time by fathering six children in rapid succession. In 1912 only the youngest, Harold and Dorothy, were still at home at Woodbank, Park Lane, Stockport. What had happened to the rolling acres we do not know? But, the Ashtons were still involved with Kirkham & Mannock at the time of its eventual close (see post p. 93).

Early records of Kirkham & Mannock are scarce, but it is probably following the final court order in 1912 that the business was incorporated into a limited company, becoming Kirkham & Mannock Limited (Company Registration No. 124806). Its incorporation would allow the various interests and loans to be represented by shares. These were of £1 each and deemed to be fully paid.

The difficulties of providing for seven children by William Mannock closely mirrored the difficulties in the Mellodew family following the death of James Mellodew in 1883. There were nine children to be provided for there, of which four were daughters. James Mellodew tried to provide for his children equally.

The solution in that case, after 13 years, was to incorporate the business, satisfy the interests of the sons by the issue of shares and provide for the daughters by the issue of Debentures, being mortgages on the company's assets. This provided its own difficulties when the company wished to borrow money from the bank, which required security. Further difficulty arose when one of the sons died, leaving income only from his shares to female offspring who pressed for income when the company was not really in a financial position to pay dividends out. By paying out most of those interested, Kirkham & Mannock avoided these difficulties.

The management of William Mannock's estate had not been without other controversy. Arthur Watts Newton of Belgrave Road, Oldham, had been appointed as an executor and trustee. How he upset the family we do not know. But, amongst family papers is a copy of a writ issued on 16 December 1890 in the Chancery Palatine Court applying that he should be removed as a trustee of the estate. This was issued on behalf of only four of the children; presumably the application was not granted as Mr Newton appears on the later court applications mentioned above.

The interests of John Mannock, William Mannock (Junior), Emma Jackson and Sarah Mannock having been paid out, little further was heard of the first three.

John Mannock remained 'living on his own means' with his wife and two stepchildren in Failsworth, dying in 1928 aged 75.

William Mannock (Junior), married at the time of his father's death to Esther from Derbyshire, gave his occupation as a farmer in the 1891 Census. His share of his inheritance having been paid out, by the time he made his will on 7 April 1900, he was able to describe himself as a 'Gentleman'. By the time of his death, he appears to have been a widower with no children. He seems to have led a rather nomadic life, farming outside Rochdale, then moving to Wirksworth (Derbyshire), making his will in Newcastle-upon-Tyne and dying in the Whitby area aged 64 in September 1918. However, he did the decent thing – leaving his estate to the children of his sisters, Emma Jackson, Alice Green Holden and Hannah Ashton. He had appointed Ralph Holden and Isaac Prockter as his executors but as both had predeceased him, his estate was administered by others.

Sarah remained unmarried and had no children. Further comment is made about her later.

These men of business obviously continued to run Kirkham & Mannock, together with their other interests, although the bulk of the work would have fallen on Ralph Holden, whose wife had a major interest in the company.

The onset of the First World War in September 1914 must have been a worrying time. The initial uncertainty caused by war however soon gave way to a requirement for cloth. Spinners were busy as never before, although a shortage of workers put pressure on wages. However the effect of war on prices was very marked. Yarn which had been selling at 7 pence (in old money) per pound weight in 1914 was up to 37 pence (in old money) per pound weight by 1917.

It is unfortunate that neither Ralph Holden nor Isaac Prockter was to see the benefit of this huge increase. Whilst it was to their respective family's advantage that they had sorted out the interests of their father-in-law, they must be given credit for actually having done so. It was certainly easier that the company no longer had so many persons interested in its future.

Ralph Holden and Isaac Prockter were to die within eight months of each other in 1916, aged 65 and 73 respectively. Their deaths require other chapters.

CHAPTER FIVE

Death of Mr Ralph Holden (1916): a diversity of interests

R ALPH HOLDEN DIED A wealthy man when he passed away at his home West Bank, 64 Napier Street East, Werneth, Oldham on 24 March 1916, aged 65. He had been taken ill about Christmas the previous year and had been confined to his room since. His will was only made shortly before his death, on 24 February. He was buried at Chadderton Cemetery, Oldham.

He was survived by his wife and five children, details of whom are given in later chapters.

His estate consisted of shares in 60 different companies, the shareholdings ranging in value from £12 to £3,755. In addition, through his interest as a partner in the firm of Waterhead Conveyancing Company he had an interest in warehouse and stable premises at Garden Street, Mumps and Waste Street, Oldham. There were also warehouse premises at Roscoe Street, two houses in Albert Street, 13 cottages at Holden Fold, Royton (with a barn and nearly 11 acres of agricultural land), a loan account with Simeon Holden Limited and a 8/45 interest in Simeon Holden's estate which consisted of ten houses at New Earth Street, Oldham and 35 houses at Marsh Street, Jackson Street, March Square and Bank Hill Street, Oldham.

The number of houses would suggest an estate of great value, but in fact most cottages were valued at something in the order of £30 each, their annual rental value at the time.

In total, the gross estate (before deduction of funeral expenses and other liabilities) amounted to £50,337, a sum equal to just over £3 million today. His 500 shares in Kirkham & Mannock Limited were valued at a mere 110p each. Where there were shares in a private company, as here, the value at the date of death was negotiated with the Estate Duty Office; the estate naturally argued for a low value as that meant less tax, and a minority shareholding, as was the case here, further reduced the valuation. The finalised value, multiplied by the total number of shares, did not therefore necessarily reflect the full worth of the company.

The estate is illustrative of the sort of shareholdings held by a wealthy Oldham man at that time – largely shares in local enterprises of which he had knowledge, and whose mill buildings he could see. This was before the time of international and large companies that we see today quoted on the London Stock Exchange.

Because of the large number of trading companies in Oldham, the town had its own stock exchange. Formally established in November 1875 as the Lancashire Share Brokers Association (changing its name to the Oldham Stock Exchange in May 1929) it had 50 founder members. From 1883 the Exchange operated from rented rooms in the Lyceum Building on Union Street, at the centre therefore of Oldham's commercial district.

The *Oldham Evening Chronicle* estimated that in the 1870s (prior to the formation of the Exchange) about 10,000 of the town's inhabitants held shares in local companies. Whilst shares changed hands privately and shares were sold by public auction, after 1875 they could also be traded on the Exchange and it is clear that the Exchange became increasingly important to local people. It is said that at one time nearly 240 local cotton mill companies were listed on the Oldham Exchange and indeed by 1893 the *Oldham Evening Chronicle* published a weekly list of quotations covering two pages.

To Close a Trust.

Important Sale of valuable Cotton Spinning, Brewery, and other Shares.

TO BE SOLD BY AUCTION by Messrs. ALLEN MELLOR & CO., at the Baptist School, Union-street West, Oldham, on THURSDAY, the 9th day of May, 1912, at 7 45 o'clock in the evening prompt, the following SHARES, subject to the Conditions of Sale to be then and there produced:—

Lot No.	No. Shares	Name of Company	Nominal Value £ s.	Paid Up £ s. d.
1	50	Lark Spinning Co. Ltd.	5 0	2 0 0
2	60	Duke Spinning Co. Ltd.	4 0	1 10 0
3	145	Ivy Spinning Co. Ltd.	5 0	2 0 0
4	56	Honeywell Spinning Co. Ltd.	5 0	3 0 0
5	550	Borough Spinning Co. Ltd.	5 0	2 0 0
6	70	Empire Spinning Co. Ltd.	5 0	2 10 0
7	180	Don Spinning Co. Ltd.	5 0	2 0 0
8	250	Fernhurst Spinning Co. Ltd.	5 0	1 2 6
9	30	Gartsides Brewery (Ordinary)	10 0	Fully
10	54	do. do. (Preference)	10 0	Fully
11	100	Boundary Spinning Co. Ltd.	4 10	1 10 0
12	200	Glodwick Spinning Co. Ltd.	5 0	2 0 0
13	100	Asia Mill Co. Ltd.	5 0	1 0 0
14	660	Prince of Wales Spinning Co.	5 0	3 0 0
15	100	Mona Mill Ltd.	5 0	1 0 0
16	382	Rock Spinning Co. Ltd.	5 0	3 0 0
17	100	Cape Spinning Co. Ltd.	5 0	1 0 0
18	1,000	Meters Ltd. (Ordinary)	1 0	Fully
19	1,410	do. do. (Preference)	1 0	Fully
20	150	Manchester Ship Canal Co. Ltd. (Ordinary)	10 0	Fully
21	40	Duchess Spinning Co. Ltd.	5 0	2 10 0
22	250	Parkside Spinning Co. Ltd.	5 0	2 0 0
23	20	Empress Brewery Co. Ltd. (Preference)	10 0	Fully
24	34	Broadway Spinning Co. Ltd.	5 0	Fully
25	350	Marlborough Spinning Co. Ltd.	5 0	2 7 6
26	365	Delta Spinning Co. Ltd.	5 0	0 10 0
27	50	Dowry Spinning Co. Ltd.	4 0	1 10 0

The number of shares in any lot may be divided at the vendor's option.

For further particulars apply to the Auctioneers, 21, Queen-street, Oldham (Tel. 318), or to Messrs. B. Grime & Son, Accountants, Prudential Buildings, Oldham (Tel. 127y), or to

FRED MEGSON, Solicitor,
26, Clegg-street, Oldham (Tel. 111x).

17. Example of shares sold by auction in Oldham in 1912

18. Oldham
Lyceum building
and façade
inscription (2016)

Mr Holden would therefore have been able to pick up shareholdings in a large number of companies relatively easily. Because of the number of worker-shareholders, small parcels of shares would regularly become available. Such holdings would be attractive to an investor businessman for the information their accounts would divulge. This probably accounts for the large number of Ralph Holden's holdings, rather than any desire to diversify his portfolio!

It is clear that Ralph Holden had been prosperous, enabling him to put together such a large estate. There are no accounts for Kirkham & Mannock Limited for this period, but figures from other Lancashire textile companies suggest that after a difficult few years at the start of the century, the years immediately prior to World War I gave rewarding results. In 1911, for instance, Thomas Mellodew & Co. Limited started to pay off the arrears of preference share dividends which had been outstanding since 1900. And then there was the profitability of war, already referred to.

It is of interest to list the shareholdings. Not only does it give an indication of the number of cotton textile companies in Oldham of which these are only a few; it also illustrates how in 1916, most shares were only partly paid up. So, a five pound share might be issued on the basis that only £2.50 be paid up. The rate of dividend would be declared on the five pounds, so that for investors there was the element of gearing up. The downside was that if a company required more capital it could 'call' on its shareholders to pay up the shares. In our example that would require a further £2.50 per share. In the event that the shareholder could not meet the call, the shares would be forfeited. As mentioned later, this became a problem in the 1920s and 1930s.

All the shareholdings below are of partly paid shares, except where indicated:

Albany Spinning Co. Limited	
Belgian Mills Co. Limited	fully paid
Borough Spinning Co. Limited	
Boundary Spinning Co. Limited	
Butler Green Spinning Co. Limited	fully paid
Bank Top Spinning Co. Limited	
Cape Spinning Co. Limited	
Central Mill Co. Limited	
Copster Mill Co. Limited	
Cairo Mill Co. Limited	
Clyde Chamber and Warehouse Trust	
Don Mill Co. Limited	
Egmont Spinning Co. Limited	
Gorse Mill Co. Limited	
Globe Spinning and Manufacturing Co. Limited	
Gem Mill Co. Limited	
Grange Mill Co. Limited	
Green Lane Spinning Co. Limited	fully paid
Henshaw Street Spinning Co. Limited	
Hurst Mill Co. Limited	fully paid
Holyrood Spinning Co. Limited	
Holly Spinning Co. Limited	
Hartford Mill Co. Limited	
Kirkham & Mannock Limited	fully paid
Asa Lees & Co. Limited	fully paid

Lees Brook Spinning Co. Limited
Lees Union Mill Co. Limited
Lime Mill Co. Limited
Lion Spinning Co. Limited   fully paid
London City and Midland Bank Limited
Maple Mill Co. Limited
New Pegamoid Limited
Nile Spinning Co. Limited
Northmoor Spinning Co. Limited
Osborne Mill Co. Limited
Oldham Velvet Manufacturing Co. Limited   fully paid
Oldham Waste Dealers Insurance Co.
Oldham Freemasons Hall Co. Limited   fully paid
Orb Spinning Co. Limited
Owl Spinning Co. Limited
Park and Sandy Lane Mills Co. Limited
Palatine Bank Limited
Pearl Mill Co. Limited
Prince of Wales Spinning Co. Limited
J. J. Rigby Limited   fully paid
Shaw Spinning Co. Limited
Smallbrook Spinning Co. Limited
Stanley Spinning Co. Limited
Shiloh Spinning Co. Limited
Thornham Spinning Co. Limited
Vine Spinning Co. Limited   fully paid
Workington Iron Co. Limited   fully paid

It was perhaps not surprising that the estate did not include the deceased's residence at 64 Napier Street East. This is because it was owned by Kirkham & Mannock Limited to whom Mr Holden had paid rent of £21 per quarter; it was quite usual for a mill to own its directors' houses.

The will made no provision for the deceased's wife Alice, presumably because Mr Holden was satisfied that she had sufficient means of her own, by reason of her inheritance from the Mannock estate, and what he might have passed to her. He left his 'jewellery, trinkets and personal ornaments' to his five children equally. As a reminder that such a bequest is likely to catch the eye of the taxman, the Inland Revenue duly asked for an account. The value of £20 attracted legacy tax of four shillings (ie. 20p)

The remainder of the estate was left equally between the five children, but, as was usual for the time, on the basis that the shares of his two daughters (Alice Mellodew and Gertrude Parker) should be retained by his trustees and the income from such shares be paid to the daughters concerned.

In leaving his daughters income only, Mr Holden was following convention. Women could own assets in their own name but it was usual to leave assets in trust for them to receive the income, rather than give them the capital. This ensured that a spendthrift husband could not get his hands on the money. It also meant that the capital went to the daughter's children, rather than to the children of a husband's second marriage, in the event that the daughter predeceased her husband.

19. Inland Revenue assessment for estate duty on jewellery in Ralph Holden's estate

Mr Holden had an income in the order of £5,441 (approximately £326,500 today) in the last year of his life. After death duties levied on his estate, his two daughters could each expect to enjoy income of approximately £1,000 per annum (approximately £60,000 today) provided dividends remained constant. The proportionate share of capital would pass to their respective children on their own deaths.

Probate of the will was granted to sons John Holden and Robert Holden on 6 September 1916. William Mannock Holden was named as an executor, but chose not to prove the will. After all he would reason, two executors were enough – why have the hassle! This accords with the general character of 'Uncle Willie'. It is perhaps not surprising that probate took some six months to obtain. It was wartime, and it is clear from the amendments later made to the estate that there was some difficulty in establishing exactly what the deceased owned. The account in relation to the jewellery, for instance, was not submitted until April 1918.

An estate with such varied interests is bound to cause difficulty; while shareholdings can be divided between beneficiaries (or the trusts), this is not the case where there are land and buildings. Unless the properties are sold, and the proceeds divided, there are inevitably going to have to be ongoing accounts dealing with the rents and repairs, and the properties require to be managed. Added to the accounts that would have to be prepared for the daughters' trust funds, there would appear to have been some good accountants' fees in prospect – accounts for the properties continued to be prepared until 1948!

A reminder that it was wartime comes from the endorsement on the grant of probate limiting those to whom assets could be distributed. Although not relevant in this case, it was a reminder nonetheless that there was a war on.

Mrs Alice Green Holden, Ralph's widow, remained at West Bank, 64 Napier Street East, Oldham. She died on 8 March 1924 aged 73 and was also buried in Chadderton Cemetery.

Her will was in similar form to her husband's; it left her estate equally between her five children but the daughters to have income only from their share, the capital of their respective one fifth share to go to their own children when they died. And so, a further two trusts were created!

Her estate amounted to £42,718 (approximately £1.7 million today). It was very conservative in content compared to her late husband's estate. It held £18,980 in government securities. The bulk of the remainder was in local companies, including 2595 shares in Kirkham & Mannock Limited, valued at 175p each as compared with 110p some eight years earlier. This reflected the substantial improvement in the trading climate both during and after the war. Indeed, for many companies, the profitability of 1920 was never to be surpassed.

Thus, the three sons received 519 shares each in Kirkham & Mannock Limited, the balance being retained in the daughters' trust. The daughters could expect to receive about £900 per annum each (approximately £36,000 today) from their mother's estate, provided of course that Kirkham & Mannock Limited continued to pay a satisfactory dividend. Added to the income being received from their father's estate, this put them each in a very comfortable position.

In His Majesty's High Court of Justice.

This Grant is made upon the condition that no portion of the assets shall be distributed or paid during the War to any beneficiary or creditor who is a German, Austro-Hungarian, Turkish or Bulgarian subject, wherever resident, or to anyone on his behalf, or to or on behalf of any person resident in Germany, Austria-Hungary, Turkey or Bulgaria, of whatever nationality, without the express sanction of the Crown, acting through the Treasury; and if any distribution or payment is made contrary to this condition the Grant of Probate or Letters of Administration will be forthwith revoked.

Upon an application to the Solicitor to the Treasury there will be no difficulty in proper cases in obtaining the sanction of the Treasury to the payment of a moderate sum out of assets to beneficiaries or creditors who are German, Austro-Hungarian, Turkish or Bulgarian subjects resident in this country at the commencement of the War and during the War.

A. MUSGRAVE,

Senior Registrar.

(6892). Wt.32,944—22. 30,000. (4). 10/15. Gp.133. A.&S.W.

20. Restriction endorsed on grants of probate in the First World War

CHAPTER SIX

A matter of pressing concern

I N ADDITION TO RUNNING the business of Prockter & Co. Limited at Vale Mill, Hollinwood, and being involved with the business of Kirkham & Mannock as an executor of William Mannock's estate along with his brother in law Ralph Holden, Isaac Prockter was a keen adherent to the Church of St Margaret, Hollinwood.

Then, as now, this was a church with high Anglican leanings. Indeed the 2016 website states that 'all our worship is in the catholic tradition with a daily mass'.

The old church of St Margaret of Antioch, to give the church its full name, was consecrated in 1769 but by the 1870s was deemed to be too small for its expanding congregation and to be unsafe. A new church was planned, built at a cost of £11,660 and consecrated in September 1879. At first it lacked a tower, but this was subsequently built in 1906. The church is impressive in structure and Grade II listed.

The clock from the old church had been stored at nearby Vale Mill and was installed in the new tower at the expense of Isaac Prockter in memory of his brother Thomas, a former churchwarden, who had died in May 1880 aged just 46.

Isaac also gave the bells in memory of his father and mother, Bartholomew and Mary Prockter, and his late sister Ellen Mellalieu, who had died in 1900 aged 53.

Living away from St Margaret's at Napier Street East did not lessen Mr Prockter's interest in the church, and a pressing matter now arose – his own burial.

It was his very particular wish that he should be buried in the churchyard of St Margaret's and he had identified a suitable spot. There was however a difficulty. The churchyard had been declared closed to new entrants. Even though there was a space available, the building of a new vault, such as Mr

Prockter wanted, would require an amendment to the order in Council of July 1899 which had decreed the closure. This meant application to the Privy Council but Mr Prockter thought this would be a formality.

Mr Prockter approached his vicar and through him application was made to the bishop.

The bishop's secretary (not the bishop!) replied rather curtly to say that the churchyard was closed to new entrants and nothing further could be done. This was not the reply that Mr Prockter wanted and he resented that a secretary, rather than the bishop, had replied to his vicar's letter. The vicar was instructed that he must write again. This time he was asked to show his proposed letter to Mr Prockter beforehand.

So the letter, as originally drafted, started with 'Dear Bishop' now became 'My dear Lord Bishop'. Sundry references were made to the generosity of Mr Prockter to St Margaret's and to connections between the Prockter family and the church. The bells, repairs to the tower and the clock were all mentioned.

The letter to the bishop was passed on to the Local Government Board in Whitehall. Their reply dated 13 August 1915, alas, was quite clear – 'the

21. St Margaret's Church, Hollinwood

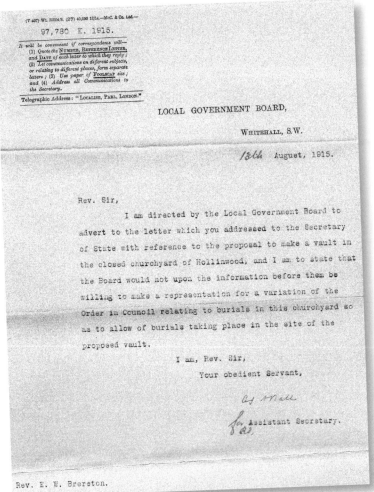

22. Letter of Refusal to the vicar of St Margaret's – 13 August 1915

Board would not be willing to make representation for a variation of the Order … to allow of burials taking place in the site of the proposed vault'. The Reverend Brereton of St Margaret's was advised by the bishop's secretary to accept the position.

Isaac Prockter was not a man to give up. He hadn't made his money by taking 'no' for an answer. The vicar was pressed to write to the bishop again. One sensed that the vicar was getting a little exasperated by pressure from his demanding parishioner. His letter of 25 August 1916 to the bishop explained that Mr Prockter had been a real benefactor to the church and, rather desperately one senses, asked 'if your Lordship would feel disposed to use your influence'.

This time the reply came from the War Trade Department. The secretary to Lord Emmott wrote that the Local Government Board had prepared a memorandum, a copy of which he enclosed, and went on to say that 'nothing less than reasons of a semi-public nature would be sufficient grounds' to proceed with the application. A reminder was given that the Local Government Board 'are particularly anxious at this moment not to be involved in the expenses connected with an official inspection and enquiry'. Mr Prockter was advised not to press the matter until after the war.

Mr Brereton, in enclosing the letter and memorandum to Mr Prockter, said 'it seems that we can do nothing further until the end of the War'.

Mr Prockter was made of sterner stuff than his vicar. In any event he was now 72, in declining health, and had his own war to fight!

The memorandum, he felt, gave grounds for hope for it said '... in certain cases, if the applicant is a person of eminence connected with the parish, or if there is a general desire to secure interment in the churchyard and adequate reasons are shown for the existence of the desire, the Board have been willing to consider the matter'.

Not only did the memorandum give grounds for hope but it had come from the War Trade Department headed by Lord Emmott. It was time to pull strings for Lord Emmott and his family had connections with Oldham.

Alfred Emmott, after a good Quaker education, had entered his father's mill and was taken into partnership by him in 1881. This firm was what became the substantial concern of Thomas Emmott & Son Limited of Vale Mills in Clegg Street and Greaves Street, Oldham. In 1891 it was running 84,700 spindles and 1,200 looms.

Young Emmott studied in his spare time becoming a graduate of London University. He also joined the Established Church (not unusual for persons wishing to 'get on'). He became a warden at St Thomas's, Werneth.

He was obviously politically ambitious and served as a Councillor, Alderman and Mayor of Oldham, a dozen years in total, and as Mayor in 1891/92.

23. Rev E. W. Brereton, Vicar of St Margaret's

In 1899 he was elected Liberal Member of Parliament for Oldham, a seat he held until 1911 when he was elevated to the peerage as Baron Emmott of Oldham in the County Palatine of Lancaster. He remained on the Council of the Oldham Chamber of Commerce.

Alfred Emmott had served as Chairman of Ways and Means (ie. as Deputy Speaker of the House of Commons) from 1906 to 1911, and was sworn in as a member of the Privy Council in 1908. He was appointed Under Secretary of State for the Colonies in 1911, remaining there until 1914. He was First Commissioner for Works between 1914 and 1915 and Director of the War Trade Department between 1915 and 1919.

If there was anyone who could assist Isaac Prockter in getting what he wanted, it was Baron Emmott!

The name of 'Prockter' would have been known to him. James Prockter had been a Liberal Councillor at the same time as himself and both men were JPs in the town. The department store of Buckley & Prockter was known to all Oldhamers. As a member of the Oldham Chamber of Commerce he would also have known of Isaac Prockter.

Given his background, it is unlikely that Mr Prockter's missive, again submitted through the vicar, would not have been mentioned to Lord Emmott. Whatever the references to Oldham and the Prockters the letter contained, the application this time worked.

By 27 October 1916 the War Trade Department, in acknowledging Mr Brereton's letter, said that that the application had been accepted and 'Lord Emmott thought you would be glad to know that the matter is proceeding satisfactorily'.

More good news came the following day when it was confirmed that a representation had been made for the Order in Council of 1899 to be varied. This letter went on to say, tactfully, 'I am to add that in the event of the death occurring before the Order in Council is issued, the burial can proceed on the assumption that the Order will be duly made'.

Even with this safeguard in hand, the rapidly ailing Mr Prockter decided to hold on. The order was made on 6 November 1916. Isaac Prockter died nine days later aged 73 on 15 November, His brother in law Ralph Holden had died some eight months earlier. Lord Emmott died suddenly in 1926 aged 67.

Rev. Brereton left Hollinwood in 1917. The history of St Margaret's comments that 'there was little recorded about this incumbency'. Perhaps he was too exhausted with one particular matter to do much else?

AT THE COURT AT BUCKINGHAM PALACE,

The 6th day of November, 1916.

PRESENT,

THE KING'S MOST EXCELLENT MAJESTY IN COUNCIL.

WHEREAS by the Burial Act, 1855, it is, amongst other things, provided that it shall be lawful for His Majesty, by and with the advice of His Privy Council, from time to time to postpone the time appointed by any Order in Council for the discontinuance of burials, or otherwise to vary any Order in Council made under any of the Acts recited in the said Act, or under the said Act (whether the time thereby appointed for the discontinuance of burials thereunder, or other operation of such Order, shall or shall not have arrived), as to His Majesty, with such advice as aforesaid, may seem fit:

And whereas Her Majesty Queen Victoria was pleased, by Her Order in Council of the 14th day of July, 1899, to direct (amongst other things) the discontinuance of burials, with certain exceptions, in the Parish Church of Hollinwood, in the Borough of Oldham and County of Lancaster, and also in the Churchyard:

And whereas it seems fit to His Majesty, by and with the advice of His Privy Council, that the said Order in Council, so far as it relates to burials in the said Parish Churchyard of Hollinwood aforesaid, should be varied:

P C 696 (1) w

2

NOW, THEREFORE, His Majesty, by and with the advice aforesaid, is pleased to order, as it is hereby ordered, that the said Order in Council of the 14th day of July, 1899, so far as it relates to burials in the Parish Churchyard of Hollinwood, in the Borough of Oldham and County of Lancaster, be and the same is hereby varied so that, notwithstanding anything therein, it shall be lawful to bury the body of Isaac Prockter, at his decease, in a vault to be constructed in the said Churchyard, provided that the coffin shall be separately enclosed by stonework or brickwork properly cemented.

ALMERIC FITZROY.

CHAPTER SEVEN

Death of Isaac Prockter (1916) and of Mary Ellen Prockter (1932)

T HE DEATH OF ISAAC PROCKTER on 15 November 1916 aged 73 removed a second son-in-law of the late William Mannock from involvement in the firm of Kirkham & Mannock Limited. We shall look at its future management later. He was of course interred in the new vault at St Margaret's, Hollinwood.

Mr Prockter's will dated 30 April 1913 carried his desire to assist his church further. He left 25 of his shares in Manchester and County Bank Limited (valued at £222) to his daughter Charlotte Mary May Prockter with the request that she use the dividends from them for keeping in repair and winding up (but not lighting) the clock of St Margaret's Church, Hollinwood. In so far as there was any income left over this should be used for the ringing of the bells. He asked that May (as she was generally called) should make a similar provision in her own will.

As to the remainder of the will, this was relatively straightforward. He left the income from one third of his estate to his wife Mary Ellen Prockter. He must have been satisfied that she didn't need more. Like her sister next door (Mrs Alice Green Holden née Mannock), she had of course received a share of William Mannock's estate. The balance was left equally between his two daughters, the unmarried May and Ethel Sumner Holden, the wife of John Holden. The two daughters would receive the 'widow's one third' when their step-mother died.

The executors were his son-in-law John Holden then of 157, Windsor Road, Oldham, and fellow cotton spinner Richard Hoyle Jackson. Mr Prockter used the power contained in the Articles of Association of Prockter & Co. Limited to appoint, by his will, John Holden as a director of that company.

There were two bothersome difficulties in relation to the estate, which amounted to the very respectable amount of £51,061 (equivalent to just over £3 million today) and of which £13,501 was referable to his shareholding in Prockter & Co. Limited. His 500 shares in Kirkham & Mannock Limited were valued at 100p each, a surprising reduction to his late brother-in-law's equal shareholding valued at 110p per share some eight months previously. estate duty was levied at the rate of 8 per cent on the whole estate with a further 1 per cent legacy duty.

The first difficulty in the estate arose from the fact that Isaac's brother, James, who had run the department store of Buckley & Prockter, had died in early 1916, aged 78. Being a widower since 1869 and without surviving children, he had made provision for his brother. James's estate amounted to £75,000.

James's will dated 29 December 1909 left his brother the income from 6 parts out of the 24 parts into which he had divided his estate. The capital of these six parts on Isaac's death were to remain in trust for May Prockter to have the income during her lifetime, the capital going to her sister Ethel Holden on May's death. The income provision for Isaac meant that James's estate had to be finalised before Isaac's as there would be an apportionment of income from James's estate up to Isaac's own death. All this would take time.

The other difficulty in relation to Isaac's estate related to the interest he still had in his late father's estate. Bartholomew Prockter had left one seventh

25. Mr Prockter's Vault at St Margaret's, Hollinwood

A Tribute to my late Master,

Isaac Prockter, Esq.

LAMENTED friend, my heart is sore,
To think that I shall nevermore
     See thy familiar face.
For long, long years we were combined :—
With trustfulness and noble mind
     Thou filled a master's place.

Oft, when my mind was full of grief,
Thy cheering words have brought relief,
     And turned night into day.
When toiling on life's rugged road,
Thou loved to share another's load,
     And help him on his way.

With jokes and tales of various blends,
How well thou could'st amuse thy friends ;
     And drive away dull care.
Thy life had'st still another side—
In Godly work thou took a pride,
     And strove to do thy share.

Thy work is done—we see thee not,
Thy body rests in " chosen spot ; "
     Tho' much against our will.
Such men as thee we sorely miss,
But thou can'st rest assured of this,
     Thou lives in memory still.

We all must bow to God's command,
But one day we shall understand
     Why these things had to be.
The strongest tree some day must fall—
Thou leaves this message to us all,
     " Prepare to follow me."

March, 1917.   JAS. CHADDERTON.

26. 'A Tribute to my late Master'

of his estate for the benefit of his daughter Elizabeth, who was to receive the income. On her death the capital was to go between her brothers and sisters (or their respective estates), of whom Isaac was one. This potential interest in capital had to be valued, and this also took time.

In the event, Elizabeth did not die until 7 June 1936. The capital, worth £3,735 in 1902, was worth only £3,567 some 34 years later. All her brothers and sisters by that time were dead. Isaac's estate received £594.65, which passed to the two daughters. The children of one late sister received the princely sum of £84.95 each – actually still a reasonable sum in 1936, equal to something in the order of £3,398 today.

The picture one has of Isaac Prockter suggests that he was a solid Victorian businessman with high Anglican Church leanings. He had obviously worked hard, initially with his father and his brother Thomas; Prockter & Co. Limited, judging by its buildings at Vale Mill, was a substantial concern, as illustrated by the value of his shareholding worth over £810,000 in terms of today's money.

He appears also to have been a much respected employer, judging by the

'Tribute to my late Master' penned by James Chadderton in March 1917. It is interesting to note the reference to 'chosen spot' as the place of Mr Prockter's burial!

However, this solid businessman was not all business and church. He had a lighter side, taking his holidays on the Isle of Man and enjoying the music hall. It was no surprise that his estate should contain shares in Theatre Royal, Manchester and Palace and Derby Castle Limited, a theatre on the Isle of Man.

It is interesting too to note that his shareholding in Buckley & Prockter was valued at about a third less than the nominal value of the shares, suggesting that the business in 1916 was not doing well. Also, in contrast to the shareholdings in Ralph Holden's estate, Isaac Prockter had sound shareholdings in well known national companies such as Brunner Mond, Lancashire and Yorkshire Railways and Manchester and County Bank – a very different portfolio from the partly paid cotton spinning company shares of his late brother-in-law.

The death of Isaac Prockter produced a gap in management at Vale Mill. His brothers Thomas and James were already dead, he had no sons, and his brother-in-law Ralph Holden had died a few months before. John Holden, of the next generation, was the obvious successor. He was married to his daughter, Ethel, and their eldest son, Isaac Prockter Holden, was now 18.

Of course, the business could have been sold, but it is likely that it was making very good money (of which more later) and one surmises that the

27. The two daughters of Isaac Prockter – Ethel Sumner Holden and May Prockter (photo taken in August 1933)

Prockter daughters, May and Ethel, together with their step-mother Mary Ellen Prockter, were reluctant to contemplate a sale whilst it was doing so well.

In fact Mary Ellen Prockter (Isaac's widow) did not die until 4 August 1932, when she was 82. Her remains were interred in the Prockter vault at St Margaret's, Hollinwood. Her death enabled the one third of Isaac's estate from which she had enjoyed the income to go equally between her step-daughters, May Prockter and Mrs Ethel Sumner Holden, John Holden's wife.

Mary Ellen's own will dated 27 June 1930 left her estate equally between the two step-daughters (May and Ethel), the children of her late sister Alice Green Holden (5) and the children of her sister Hannah Ashton (6), a division into 13 in all.

Her gross estate amounted to over £65,000. Death duties took £10,476 but the division still gave a decent inheritance to each beneficiary. The 7594 shares she held in Kirkham & Mannock Limited were divided equally, each beneficiary receiving 584 shares. This did not bring any new shareholders on to the company's share register, as the five children of Ralph Holden, the two Prockter girls and the children of Hannah Ashton (William Mannock's daughter) were already shareholders. The shares were valued at 130p each.

All Mary Ellen's chattels were left to May, who continued to reside at 62 Napier Street East. Isaac Prockter Holden was one of the executors of the will, a post he seemed to occupy for so many later Holden estates.

But, we have run a little ahead of ourselves and it is appropriate to look at the family in 1916 and the immediate years after the First World War ended in 1918.

CHAPTER EIGHT

The golden years, the difficult years and an untimely death

WHEN RALPH HOLDEN DIED in 1916, cotton spinners generally were profiting greatly. Britain was at war and the demand for cloth was enormous. As Bowker in *Lancashire Under The Hammer* comments, '… when Governments buy in bulk, or, better still, when Governments are driven to commandeering whole factories regardless of cost, men in the know and in the swim are assured of pickings that make their richest days before seem lean'.

Tattersall's Cotton Trade Reviews for 1914 to 1918 expand on this. Of spinning in 1916 he wrote, 'The way in which users have paid exceptional rates has been surprising, and at one time it would have been thought impossible for business to be done at such enhanced values'. By 1917, Tattersall was remarking that for spinners 'the margin of profit might be very easily reduced and trade be still very remunerative'. And by 1918, Tattersall could report that 'records have been established which in pre-war days could not have been dreamed about … More money has been made than in any previous twelve months'.

The year of 1918 'was a record year for profits but 1919 has been even better', according to Tattersall, and 'it is probable that in 1920 all previous figures will be beaten'. The general view is that 1920 in terms of profit did indeed surpass all previous years.

The Mellodews of Moorside had a record year and received an offer for their business from Tootal, Broadhurst Lee & Co. Ltd in 1920. It was to come to nothing but it illustrates the vibrancy and volatility of the time.

For families such as the Holdens, the Mellodews and the Stotts and many other Oldham families these were golden years and it is not surprising that they got used to a way of life that they were later reluctant to give up.

Well to do families were beginning to buy motor cars. Many of them never

drove but they usually had a part time chauffeur, often employed by their business, who would do that. If a trip to Manchester was needed, a telephone call to the mill was made and a car and driver appeared! These families had domestic staff. The Holdens were no exception.

For the comfortably placed Oldham family, such as the Holdens, at the end of the First World War this was a good time. There was prosperity. There was easy access to Manchester, with its Opera House, shops and Midland Hotel. Oldham itself had the Coliseum Theatre (dating back to 1885), the Assembly Rooms (dances were by invitation) and The Lyceum, where the ladies went to play bridge or have tea. Children were sent away to school – Harrogate Ladies College or Queenswood, Hatfield for the girls, Repton, Rossall or Rugby for the boys.

Most of these families still lived in central Oldham – Queens Road, opposite Alexandra Park, Windsor Road and the Coppice were favoured areas. They lived in Oldham because that is where their wealth creating business was based. Whilst some families had started to move out to what were seen as the more congenial environs of South Manchester, most stayed put. It was a close-knit and prosperous community, and some satisfactory marriages were made. This was not surprising as the mill owners' children were going to the same schools, the same dances and the same tennis clubs and holiday places.

Ralph Holden had been well connected in Oldham, as his business interests and investments show. He also had the advantage that his four children that married, had all 'married well' thus widening his field of connections. Information even if received in a domestic setting could always be useful to a businessman.

29. Mr John Holden

But Ralph Holden was now dead and the family's assets needed to be maintained.

John Holden, born in 1872, was 44 at the time of his father's death. As the eldest son it was natural that he should step into his father's shoes to run Kirkham & Mannock Limited. He already had experience of the company and he lived within easy distance of the Marsland Mills, living comfortably at Brentwood, 186 Windsor Road, Oldham, which he and his wife had had built for them.

Neither of John's brothers, Robert Holden ('Bob') nor William Holden ('Willie') had shown much aptitude for the harsh realities of business, preferring instead to run the much smaller business of Simeon Holden Limited, the cotton waste dealers. They were quite content that John should run Kirkham & Mannock.

Bob, a bachelor, was still living at home at 64 Napier Street East with his mother, whilst Willie had very satisfactorily married into the Gartside family.

30. Brentwood, 186 Windsor Road, Oldham – home of Mr and Mrs John Holden

Their cousin, Robert Ashton (son of Hannah Ashton née Mannock) was a little younger than John and was already in the business; his skill was confined to the secretarial and accountancy side of the firm.

So, to John fell the responsibility of running Kirkham & Mannock Limited for the benefit of the Holden and Ashton families and his aunt, Mary Ellen Prockter.

But there was also Prockter & Co. Limited's business at Vale Mill, Hollinwood, to be managed. This was also within easy walking distance of John Holden's house. This business was being run for the benefit of his aunt, Isaac Prockter's widow, his sister in law May and his wife Ethel. But one man could not run all this.

Thus it was that John Holden's eldest son, Isaac Prockter Holden, was forced to finish his education and at the age of 18 found himself running Prockter & Co. Limited under parental supervision. It was a task that he found difficult, resenting the fact that he had not been given the opportunity to choose his own career.

We do not have any accounts for Prockter & Co. Limited, but its prosperity and difficulties probably mirrored those of Kirkham & Mannock.

After the profitable years of war, and the joyous bonanza of 1920, the years of difficulty for the cotton trade arrived. In 1921 the Indian government imposed an import duty on cotton goods of 11 per cent, increasing it to 14 per cent the following year. There was pressure in India to ban imports altogether. This had been one of Lancashire's largest markets, and the effect was to reduce the demand for yarn. I do not have the figures for Oldham, but in Blackburn the effect was to render 43,000 looms to stand idle, with an obvious knock-on effect for the spinners.

In 1921, Mahatma Gandhi was in England. He was taken to Blackburn to see what the loss of the Indian export market had done to the town. He said, 'The poverty I have seen distresses me but, compared to the poverty and pauperism of the starving millions of India, the poverty of Lancashire dwindles into insignificance'. What else could he say?

31. Isaac Prockter Holden as a schoolboy

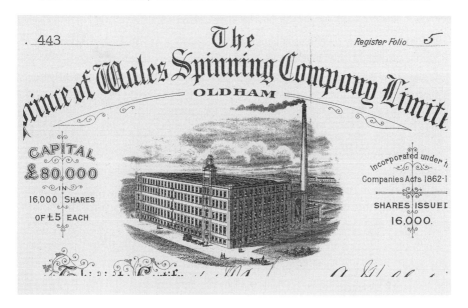

32. Impressive heading to a share certificate of The Prince of Wales Spinning Company Limited

However, Kirkham & Mannock Limited weathered the storm. By 1924 it was on the telephone (No. 131), still had its same telegraphic address of 'Lion, Oldham' and had made a sufficient profit to pay a dividend of 19.5p per share.

The year 1926 saw the emergence of the General Strike, and mill owners were fearful of the damage that might be caused by the unrest.

The General Strike of 1926 came about because after several weeks of negotiation the miners' union rejected the demands of the coal owners for longer hours and reduced wages. The suggested wages were so low that the miners viewed the offered sums as tantamount to a lock out. The request had been made because of falling coal exports as prices rose when Britain returned to the Gold Standard in 1925. The miners appealed to the government to put pressure on the coal owners, but to no avail. The TUC called a General Strike in the belief that the threat would induce the government to change its mind and intervene. The government refused, so the General Strike started on 4 May 1926. It lasted nine days before the TUC backed off; the miners remained on strike for another five months before they drifted back to work.

There is no evidence that the strike affected the Marsland Mills. Either the mills had adequate stocks of coal for their steam engines or, like the Mellodews, they were able to obtain supplies without too much difficulty.

In any event, for the year ended 1926 they were able to pay an increased dividend of 25p per share.

Business obviously became tougher thereafter. The payment for 1929 was reduced to 18.75p per share, rising to 19.35p for 1931, but then falling to 13.33p per share in 1933.

This was a bad time. As the miners had found out, wages were reduced because of the state of trade. A wage of £1 per week on the standard list in 1910 rose steadily until May, 1920, when the industry was at its peak of profitability, to the high figure of £5.77. A series of reductions was to follow until 1932, which brought the rate down to only 62p or just over 60 per cent of the 1910 rate. It was not until October 1940 that it recovered to its 1910 level and 1963 before it reached its May 1920 peak.

William Woodruff in his book *The Road to Nab End* reports that by 1931 there were three million unemployed and the cotton industry had reached a state of collapse. This was a time of political upheaval. There was a reduction in unemployment benefit, income tax was increased from 20p to 23p in the £1 and super tax was increased too. By August 1931 a Labour government had been replaced by a national government with Ramsay MacDonald as Prime Minister and a general election was to be held in October. By 1932 it was generally agreed that Britain had slipped into the depths of a depression.

In the midst of all this political confusion, Aunt Sarah Mannock died on 11 September 1931, aged 70. Her will of 13 October 1930 was surprising in that there was no acknowledgement of the existence of the Holden or Ashton families. Family recognition was limited to the children and grandchildren of her sister, Emma Jackson, who received by way of legacies approximately half her estate, with the residue amounting to just under £5,000 going equally to Oldham Royal Infirmary and Henshaw's Blue Coat School, Oldham. Sarah was entitled to the income from one seventh of William Mannock's estate, which had been put into a separate trust fund following the 1891 court hearing. This capital was now to be distributed in similar terms to her own will. It is not known how much this might have been.

Aunt Sarah had used Mr Arthur Slater, a solicitor not generally used by the Prockter and Holden families, to make her will. And, the executors were not family either, being James Newton, a spinning company secretary, Thomas Collins, a hay and straw dealer, and Mr Slater. It could be that James Newton was related to Arthur Watts Newton, an executor of the late Mr William Mannock's estate all those years ago, and who had lived in Belgrave Road.

Whatever the position, in the immediate short term, it might have been felt that there had been a 'slip up' in communication for there to have been no monetary acknowledgement of the Holden and Ashton families. Perhaps Aunt Sarah felt that the time she had spent looking after her father Mr William Mannock, had not been properly appreciated? Perhaps she felt that the Holdens and the Prockters had been too comfortable compared to her?

Sarah's sister, Mary Ellen Prockter, as we have seen, was to die the following year. She left most of her estate to the children of her two other sisters, so it could be that there was no 'slip up', the sisters taking the view that between them they would divide their assets between their respective sisters' children, of whom the Holdens formed part. We shall not know.

Aunt Sarah's death was however merely a distraction to the ongoing life of the Holden family and the affairs of Kirkham & Mannock Limited, where the difficulties of the cotton industry were cause for concern.

The *Oldham Chronicle* for 14 May 1932 made grim reading. It listed the surplus capacity in the cotton trade. It revealed that Ram Mill at Hollinwood, one of the most modern and up-to-date mills in the district with 112,980 mule spindles, had been offered for sale by Order of the Court and had received only two bids – of just £5,000 and £10,000. Lily Mill had made a call on its shareholders and Mavis Mill had been closed since October.

The well known Prince of Wales Spinning Co. Limited now made a call on its shareholders, as did The Ruby Mill Company Limited (1931 and 1932) and Peel Mills Limited (1932 and 1935). Calls on partly paid shares became a problem for those holding them for such calls required cash, and cash was in short supply for many. This was not helped by the financial collapse of a mill company whose capital had been supplied by way of loans, often from its own workers and local people.

This was a time when, as reported in *The Shiloh Story 1874–1974* many hundreds of families were ruined. 'Those who had loaned money to the mills found out that their loans were totally unsecured. Those who were shareholders were called to pay up the unpaid capital. Those who were both loan holders and shareholders were not able to set their loan money against their calls. Not only did shareholders and loan holders suffer but from 1921 until 1937 the operatives were compelled to accept substantial reductions in wage rates. During the same period there were long periods of unemployment and organised short time working'.

Dividends were cut by Lion Spinning, Thornham Spinning, Vine Spinning and Oldham Velvet. Private companies were not immune. Thomas Mellodew & Co. Limited halved the dividend on its ordinary shares in 1931, halved it again in 1934 before ceasing to pay dividends at all. Kirkham & Mannock Limited were no exception to straitened times and dividends were reduced

The Prince of Wales Spinning Co. Ltd.

Capital £80,000 in 16,000 Shares of £5 each, £5 per Share paid up.

Call of £2 per Share.

No. of Shares _____ *335*

Amount Called £ _____ *670*

To Mr. James A. Kelloden.

30TH JULY, 1932.

DEAR SIR OR MADAM,

I beg to give you notice that at a Meeting of the Directors of the Company, held here on the 27th day of July, 1932, a Call of Two Pounds (£2) per Share was made, and it was determined that such Call should be paid to the Company at the Registered Office at the Mill, or to the Company's Bankers, Midland Bank Limited, Union Street, Oldham, or any Branch of the said Bank, by the instalments and on the dates following, viz. :—

10s. 0d. on the 27th day of October, 1932.
10s. 0d. on the 27th day of January, 1933.
10s. 0d. on the 27th day of April, 1933.
10s. 0d. on the 27th day of July, 1933.

The sum payable by you in respect of the _____ *335* _____ Shares, of which you are the holder, is £ _____ *670* _____, and I have to request that you will pay the same in accordance with this notice as follows :—

On or before the 27th day of October, 1932, the sum of £ *164. 10. 0*
On or before the 27th day of January, 1933, the sum of £ *164. 10. 0*
On or before the 27th day of April, 1933, the sum of £ *164. 10. 0*
On or before the 27th day of July, 1933, the sum of £ *164. 10. 0*

When all the Instalments have been paid, this letter, together with Share Certificate, should be sent to the Company for endorsement of the Call paid.

Under the Articles of Association of the Company, interest at the rate of £5% per annum must be paid upon any portion of the Call which is not paid on or before the due date.

By Order of the Board of Directors,

HERBERT LEES,

Registered Office :—   Secretary.

VULCAN STREET,
OLDHAM.

33. Letter of Call from Prince of Wales Spinning Co. Limited – 30 July 1932

progressively from 1931 through most of the '30s. However, a dividend payment, even if reduced, continued to be paid, which suggests either adequate reserves or continuing profits.

Kirkham & Mannock Limited shares were fully paid and there was no necessity to call upon its shareholders for further funds.

John Holden, recognising the volatility of the time and the inherent risks associated with the cotton trade, wisely had spent time repositioning his own and his wife's portfolios. He had largely disposed of his late father's holdings of partly paid shares so there were no great demands for cash from struggling cotton firms landing on the Brentwood doorstep.

So in spite of these difficult times, the Holdens were able to lead a comfortable life. John Holden and his wife now both had money invested outside the cotton trade, Kirkham & Mannock was still paying a dividend, and they had other assets. They lived in their own large and comfortable home, Brentwood, 186 Windsor Road, Oldham, and their family was becoming settled.

Their eldest son Isaac Prockter Holden, born in 1898, had married on 6 September 1923, and a granddaughter, Barbara, was born on 28 April 1929.

Their other son, John ('Jack') was very satisfactorily married to Kitty Stott (not related to the James Stott family mentioned in Chapter Eleven but still a satisfactory match as Kitty Stott's family made meters and measuring devices and a great deal of money!). Their son, John Vernon Holden, was born on 26 September 1931. Isaac and his wife lived next door to his parents and Jack and his family lived nearby at 304 Windsor Road.

For young people whose family had money, a jolly time could still be had, in spite of political and financial uncertainty. There were dances at the Union

34. Isaac Prockter Holden and Margaret Whiteside on their wedding day (1923)

Club and at the Park Lawn Tennis Club, Oldham, and further afield at the Midland Hotel, Manchester. Obviously stamina was needed – first supper was at 10pm and second supper at 11.15pm. Chauffeurs would be on hand with the cars, so there were no drink driving rules to worry about. Nannies could take care of the children and maids would see to the household chores. Of course, all this had to be arranged and supervised, but it made for a civilised life.

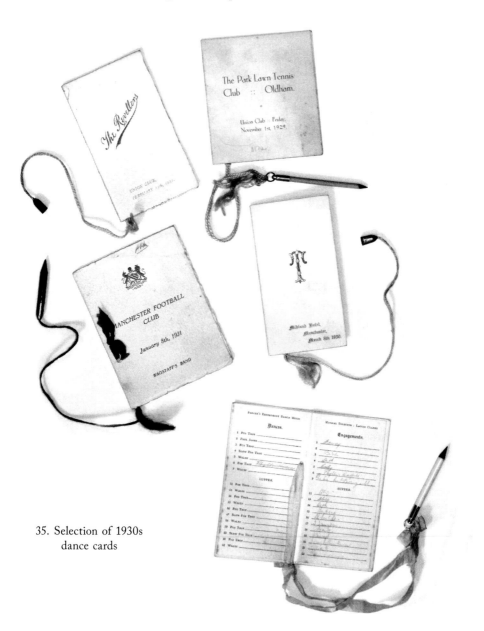

35. Selection of 1930s
    dance cards

In the midst of all this, John Holden died, aged 61. His death on Christmas Day 1933 must have been awkward, to say the least. Like his parents, he was buried at Chadderton Cemetery, Oldham, the funeral taking place on 28 December – a pretty miserable Christmas?

He left a very creditable estate of £85,038 (equal to something in the order of £3.4 million today). His widow, Ethel, was left the right to live in Brentwood and to use the contents, and this she did. She was also left the income from one third of her husband's estate. This 'widow's third' was to pass to her sons on her death.

The remaining capital passed to the two sons, Isaac and Jack. Ethel clearly had sufficient money of her own not to need the income from the whole of her husband's estate. The arrangement would limit the incidence of estate duty on her own death, by keeping the value of her estate down.

It is interesting to compare the investments in John Holden's estate with those of his father in 1916 from which John had received a one fifth share. There are still a number of shareholdings in local mills, but a significant number of shareholdings in large national companies – British American Tobacco, Cable and Wireless, Imperial Chemical Industries, Martins Bank, Manchester Ship Canal and Vickers Limited together with fixed interest holdings in railway companies and £36,000 in government stock. This represents a very real change of emphasis since his father's day. Only one of the mill shareholdings is shown as partly paid. The schedule does disclose that six shareholdings, including Prockter & Co. Limited were not paying dividends – a sign of the times. His 3277 shares in Kirkham & Mannock Limited were valued at just under 120p each.

This change in investments since his father's time to those existing at his own death shows great acumen by John Holden. He had obviously recognised that the future of the cotton trade was likely to be difficult. He had moved his assets from risky volatile enterprises to solid publicly quoted companies. His sons had cause to be grateful.

The total income produced by his portfolio was £2,400, a poor return given its size, but as mentioned above, there was other income so he would have been able to manage comfortably.

Untidily, his estate still included interests in his father's estate (died 1916), his mother's estate (died 1924) because of properties retained, and an interest in the estate of his aunt Mary Ellen Prockter, who had died the previous August.

Still, his death created a vacuum at the mills and the next generation had to step forward.

CHAPTER NINE

A consolidation of assets, activity in World War II, and a withdrawal from business

T HEIR FATHER WAS ONLY 61 when he died and he had retained the reins of power. His death required Isaac (then aged 35) and Jack (then aged 30) to fully take over the running of Prockter & Co. Limited at Vale Mill and Kirkham & Mannock Limited at Marsland Mills. Isaac, as the eldest son, was already supervising Vale Mill, regarded possibly as the family's premier mill, owing to its size.

Fortunately, Isaac and Jack got on, although Isaac's family always felt that Jack had been the favoured son, being the youngest. When Isaac was 21, he was given a bicycle. When Jack was 21, he was given a car! However, this did not stop them holidaying together and getting on.

Both sons now had money from their father's estate and both were married, each with one child.

In Jack's case, his marriage to Kitty Stott meant that she had money too. Unfortunately, Kitty suffered from depression from time to time. Some of this was so severe that she was given what was called 'electric shock treatment' thought to be a cure at the time. This was to have no effect.

Neither of the uncles was interested in running the two mills. Robert Holden ('Uncle Bob') and William Mannock Holden ('Uncle Willie') were running the cotton waste merchant business of Simeon Holden Limited in a half-hearted way as it was already running down. Uncle Bob was coming up to 60 and, like Willie, had money from his parents' estates.

Simeon Holden Limited was finally wound up on 4 May 1939, the leasehold premises having been sold and total realisations of £7,304 paid out (largely repayment of loan accounts).

36. Jack Holden's wedding
to Kitty Stott (1927)

The family was well entrenched on Windsor Road. Mrs Ethel Holden (John's widow) was living at Brentwood (No. 186), Isaac's family was at Lyncroft, 188 Windsor Road and Uncle Willie, Auntie May and daughter Joan were at No. 190. Uncle Bob was still at 64 Napier Street East. Jack and Kitty Holden were living at 304 Windsor Road, but by 1942 had moved to 'Beverley', Selkirk Avenue, within easy walking distance of both Brentwood and the Marsland Mills. Ralph Holden's two daughters Auntie Gertie Parker and Alice Maud Mellodew were in Royton and Dunham Massey, outside Altrincham, respectively.

This meant that the family was in close contact and close knit. Ethel Holden fostered this cohesion by holding a large party in 1935 for all the children in the related families. Not only her grandchildren, but the Ashton and Jackson infants were present. With conjurors and other entertainers, lots of jellies and other treats, the 50 or so children must have had a marvellous time.

But in spite of this settled state of affairs, neither Isaac nor his brother Jack had an appetite for running a cotton spinning business. They were engineers at heart and that is where their interest lay. They found union demands

37. Mrs Ethel Holden
(John Holden's widow)

at Vale Mill (for instance in
relation to wet floors – inevitable
in the cotton industry) difficult
to cope with, however reasonable.
They also recognised that the
mill was a potential fire hazard
with highly combustible cotton
and oily surfaces. To put in a
satisfactory fire protection system,
as demanded by the Unions, would
cost many thousands of pounds.
They did not think it prudent to
put any of their own money into
updating the mills and, of course,
borrowing was out of the question.

In any event, it was difficult to make any money. When they had the
opportunity to sell, they took it. Vale Mills was sold and Prockter & Co.
Limited put into Members Voluntary liquidation. It was not until December
1941 that a first distribution was made. Ultimately shareholders received 92p
for each £1 share.

Kirkham & Mannock Limited survived the '30s and managed to pay
dividends throughout, although dropping from 13.33p per share for 1933 to

38. Isaac
Holden's house
at Lyncroft,
188 Windsor
Road, Oldham

The Prince of Wales Spinning Company Limited.

Registered Office :

VULCAN STREET,

OLDHAM.

NOTICE IS HEREBY GIVEN that an EXTRAORDINARY GENERAL MEETING of the Members of the above-named Company will be held at the Registered Office of the Company, situate in VULCAN STREET, OLDHAM, on WEDNESDAY, THE SEVENTH DAY OF APRIL, 1937, at Three o'clock in the Afternoon, for the purpose of considering and, if thought fit, passing the following Resolution as a Special Resolution :—

"That the Company be wound up voluntarily, and that Mr. Clifford "Atkins, of Prudential Buildings, Union Street, Oldham, Chartered "Accountant, be and he is hereby appointed Liquidator for the "purposes of such winding up."

Dated this 12th day of March, 1937.

By order of the Board,

HERBERT LEES,

SECRETARY.

39. Resolution for the Voluntary Liquidation of The Prince of Wales Spinning Company Limited (1937)

6.45p in 1936 before recovering to 13.79p by the end of 1939. This of course was a far cry from the dividends of 25p per share of the mid-1920s, but much better than a lot of other firms who were paying no dividend at all.

Throughout the 1930s such apparently sound firms like Asa Lees, Borough Spinning, Thornham Spinning, Vine Spinning and others all continued to cut their dividends, or pass them altogether. The Prince of Wales Spinning Co. Limited gave up completely, going into voluntary liquidation, whilst it was solvent, in 1937. As we have seen, Prockter & Co. Limited followed a similar course.

Trading gloom though did not stop the Holdens from having a good time. Jack and Kitty spent the Christmas of 1935 at The Palace Hotel, Buxton, and appeared to have thrown themselves wholeheartedly into the fancy dress party there.

World War II started in September 1939, and there were soon shortages of cotton. There was thus only limited working in the cotton spinning industry. This was wasteful of labour and space.

The government proposed a re-organisation of the textile industry. It believed that concentrating capacity would use labour more efficiently and free space for the manufacture of munitions or for storage. The Marsland Mills of Kirkham & Mannock Limited, unlike the Mellodews, were not large or efficient enough to qualify for 'nucleus status' and thereby receive guaranteed supplies of cotton. It was therefore directed by government to manufacture munitions.

A change of activity stimulated both Isaac and Jack Holden. They designed and built machinery. They set up a small workshop in the mill yard. They made bullets and parts for radar installations. The mills had three shifts working. The place was busy. This is reflected in the rise in dividend – 16.04p for 1940, 16.67p for 1941, 20p for 1942 before settling down to 15p per share for the rest of the war.

It is perhaps useful to have a reminder of income tax rates. These had risen steadily from 23p in the pound in 1931 (with falls at the time of deflation in 1933 and 1934) up to 27p for the year ending 5 April 1939. The war years saw increases to 35p in 1940, 43p in 1941 and 50p for the rest of the war and through to 1946, when rates declined to 45p for 1947, 1948 and 1949. In

40. Jack and Kitty Holden in fancy dress at The Palace Hotel Buxton (1935)

41. Isaac Prockter Holden

addition, depending on individual circumstances, there was a surtax or super tax. Increased dividends would not necessarily therefore mean the Holdens were better off in terms of spendable income!

Isaac and his brother also started a small engineering business – Kirkham & Mannock Engineers Limited – making covers for boilers. It is not known how this fared, but perhaps its liquidation in 1948 tells its own tale?

Auntie May Prockter (Charlotte Mary May Prockter) died on 17 May 1941, aged 72. She had of course inherited money from her father Isaac, and her stepmother Mary Ellen Prockter, but nevertheless her estate of £102,876 came as something of a welcome surprise.

Her will of 21 July 1939 was straightforward and short – a legacy of £250 to Oldham Royal Infirmary and the balance equally between Isaac and Jack, who were appointed executors. Estate duty at 26 per cent and legacy duty took just over £31,000 but the overall proceeds must have been nonetheless appreciated.

May's estate mainly consisted of publicly quoted shares – Imperial Chemical Industries, Wilson's Brewery, Trafford Park Estates, Lewis's Investment Trust, to name but a few. She had not invested in the numerous textile companies which still dominated the Oldham landscape. She did however hold 834 shares in Kirkham & Mannock Limited (valued at £2 each) and a large holding of ordinary shares in Prockter & Co. Limited. On finalisation of its liquidation these produced £13,710, a very gratifying increase on the amount agreed for estate duty purposes of £4,843 (with no capital gains tax!) as liquidation had not started at the time of her death.

The death of May Prockter meant that ¼ of her Uncle James Prockter's estate could now be released. He had died in 1916 and May had received income from his estate after her father's death. The capital due of £9,770 (after estate duty at 26 per cent) was now paid to her sister, Ethel Holden.

May Prockter's death also meant that 62, Napier Street East, could revert to Kirkham & Mannock Limited. Uncle Bob continued to live at no.64.

It was only a few months later that May's sister, Mrs Ethel Sumner Holden (John Holden's widow), died on 5 September 1941, aged 70. She had been ill since the previous December. A codicil to her will, dated 9 December 1940, had to be signed by her with her mark (as opposed to her signature) as she was so ill. The solicitors concerned prudently had the codicil witnessed by her doctor and a nurse to avoid any suggestion that she did not know what she was doing.

Ethel Holden too left a satisfactory estate at £97,068, attracting estate duty of £23,473 with a further charge for legacy duty. Apart from an annuity to her cousin Helen Ward of £52 per annum, she left her estate equally between her sons, Isaac and Jack, and appointed them as her executors.

Her estate was even more conservative than her sister's in its investments. Whilst she held 584 shares in Kirkham & Mannock Limited (valued at £2 each), nearly all the rest of her estate consisted of government and other fixed interest securities. It is interesting to see that she held shares in Buckley & Prockter Limited (the department store), which were deemed to be valueless. She did however hold a Debenture which, apparently, was covered by the value of the company's buildings, so was likely to be repaid her investment in due course. Prockter & Co. Limited, previously of Vale Mill, in which like her sister she had shares, was by this time in members voluntary liquidation.

It might be thought that the death of Ethel Holden would allow her husband's estate to be fully would up. She had occupied the house, Brentwood, under the terms of his will. That was sold to Park Cake Supplies Limited on 19 February 1942 for £1,700. Similarly investments of £22,000, from which she had enjoyed income, could be distributed. But, John Holden's estate still had interests under the wills of Ralph Holden and Alice Green Holden – largely property assets that had been retained – so there were to be yet further ongoing accounts.

42. Dividend payment from Kirkham & Mannock Limited – 30 June 1945

Although war continued, with Kirkham & Mannock Limited still paying dividends of 15p per share, Isaac now planned his escape from Oldham. He was secure financially, having received very approximately over £100,000 (equivalent to about £4 million today) by way of inheritances, and he now purchased a house at Woodcroft, Storrs Park, Windermere, in the grounds of Storrs Hall. Come the end of the war, he and his wife moved there.

Storrs Hall itself is now an upmarket hotel and Isaac for a time had a financial interest in it. Their Oldham house at 188 Windsor Road was sold to Uncle Bob, who unfortunately was not to live there for very long.

Windermere suited Isaac Holden. Mrs Holden disliked it. She missed the social life of Oldham and trips to Manchester. A subsequent move to Morecambe meant that they were a little less rural than at Storrs Park. The couple later moved again, this time to Howe Top, 14 Rushley Mount, Hest Bank, near Lancaster.

Uncle Bob (Robert) Holden died on 11 August 1946 aged 69. He had been ill with a heart condition. When he made his will on 30 September 1930, he had been living at the old family home of 64 Napier Street East, Oldham. Following the death of May Prockter next door, and the move of Isaac Holden to Windermere, he was probably encouraged to buy Isaac's house at 188 Windsor Road, as this was next door to his brother Willie. Following family tradition, he was buried at Chadderton Cemetery.

43. Storrs Hall, Windermere – latterly an hotel. Image courtesy of Storrs Hall Hotel, www.storrshall.com.

His move had allowed Kirkham & Mannock Limited to sell the now vacant numbers 62 and 64 Napier Street East. These houses were to become 62A, 62B, 64A and 64B Napier Street East and subsequently to become the 19 bedroomed modest 2 star High Point Hotel (see Illustration 15).

Even in 1930, Uncle Bob had described himself as a retired cotton waste dealer. There is no evidence that he did much work since, except probably 'play the Stock Exchange'. Perhaps symptomatic of this is the fact that his estate papers show that he held over 80 shareholdings. At the time of his death he had a chauffeur, William Holt (who was actually an employee of Kirkham & Mannock Limited), to whom he left £250, and a housekeeper, Mary Mellor, to whom he left an annuity of £104 per

44. Isaac Holden on Windermere

annum. Both these gifts had been made by a codicil to his will dated 2 August 1946 when he was sufficiently ill only to be able to sign his name by his mark.

The rest of his will was straightforward. His nephews Isaac, Jack and his sister Alice's son, Alan Mellodew, were appointed as executors. Surprising for a family that had already so many family trusts, with all the administration that entailed, Uncle Bob left the income from a quarter of his estate to his sister Gertrude Parker for her lifetime. He must have thought that as a widow she would be short of income. Nothing was further from the truth (see Chapter Thirteen). Subject to that, the estate was left to all his nephews and nieces (Isaac Holden, Jack Holden, Joan Holden and the children of his sister Alice, namely Alice Ramage, Alan Mellodew and Nancy Royce), six in all.

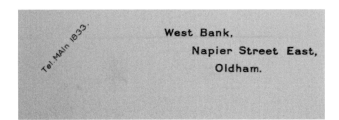

Tel. MAin 1833.

West Bank,

Napier Street East,

Oldham.

45. Uncle Bob's card from West Bank 64 Napier Street East, Oldham. House number not necessary if you were a Holden!

The Brother and Sisters
of the late Robert Holden
gratefully acknowledge and desire
to thank you for your kind
expression of sympathy in their
bereavement.

'Lyneroft'
Windsor Road,
Oldham.   *August 1946.*

46. Acknowledgement card following Uncle
Bob's death (1946)

Sufficient money was put on one side to purchase Treasury Stock, which would provide for Mary Mellor's annuity, and the 3774 shares held by Uncle Bob in Kirkham & Mannock Limited were divided equally between the six, the shares being valued at £1.63 each.

Uncle Bob's estate amounted to over £83,000 and after estate duty of £26,962 and other expenses each of the beneficiaries received shares and cash in the order of £8,000. This included the house sale proceeds, following a sale to Gerald Megson, of £4,100.

None of the beneficiaries wanted cash. They preferred shares, but given the quantity of Uncle Bob's shareholdings and the fact that some of them could not economically be divided by six, Henry Cooke & Co. stockbrokers drew up a scheme of division.

Although the portfolio included shares in leading companies, such as Dunlop, Martins Bank, British Match, ICI, Distillers and Turner & Newall, it also included shares in Bee Spinning, Belgrave Mills, Cromer Ring Mills, Fir Spinning, Melbourne, Owl, Willow Bank, Shiloh and Slack Mills spinning companies, most of which were quoted on the Oldham Stock Exchange. This somewhat mirrored the estate left by his father Ralph Holden some 30 years earlier and is in great contrast to the conservative portfolios of May Prockter and Ethel Holden. It would seem that the beneficiaries felt a close connection to Oldham mills by wishing to retain these shares.

So far as Uncle Bob's chattels were concerned, there was no informal sharing out. Perhaps there was some mistrust between the cousins? Everything had a value put on it. Even the wine in the house was sold, fetching £5. Silver was sold for £6, clothes for £15 and other personal belongings for £1. The value of anything wanted by a beneficiary was taken off their share.

Alan Mellodew had the bulk of the chattels, having recently come back from the war and having to furnish his house at Fairbank, Ripponden Road, Moorside. What was not required was sold for £622. Auntie Gertie organised all this, and was paid £240 by the estate for her trouble – including trying to get rid of the furs which Uncle Bob had obviously inherited from his mother! Alan Mellodew sold the car, an Armstrong Siddeley, for £1,139.

So, Isaac and Jack received additional assets. But there was more to come.

In February 1948, the premises at Roscoe Street and Albert Street, Mumps, included in Ralph Holden's estate were at last sold. The proceeds of £4,062 were divisible between his

48. Jack Holden

five children, or their estates. That brought that estate to an end, except for the ongoing trusts for Alice Mellodew and Gertrude Parker, which would not end until their respective deaths.

While Isaac was resident in Windermere, remaining a director and journeying to Oldham as and when required, Jack continued to run the business at Kirkham & Mannock Limited. He was a regular attender at Manchester's Royal Exchange to purchase cotton and sell yarn.

47. Oldham Stock Exchange List (extract) – 10 January 1947 – showing quotations for local mill companies

The year 1947 saw a reduction in the dividend to 13.63p per share, possibly because of a fall in production following the savage winter and coal strike of that year. But there was an increase in dividend to 15p per share in 1950. This was not an easy time. Unions were beginning to press for higher wages. Income tax was still high at 45p in the £1. Textile companies were having to reposition themselves after the war and the government was keen on vertical integration so that spinning, weaving, finishing, dyeing and merchanting could all be carried on by the same enterprise.

Emoluments for the directors remained pretty constant, rising from £1,797 for the year ended 10 December 1948 to £2,306 for the year ended 12 December 1952. Shareholders could hardly complain that the directors were taking out more in remuneration than the shareholders were receiving in dividends – a marked contrast to the complaints of the Mellodew shareholders in the 1930s.

In 1952, as The Cotton Board reported, the cotton trade suffered the shock of an extremely sharp and painful recession after 12 months of a sellers' market. There had been difficulties and problems during the war, and afterwards, – mainly lack of raw cotton – but not difficulties of selling.

Trading profit at Kirkham & Mannock for the year to December 1952 slumped to £41,755 from the very high figure of £85,162 for the year earlier.

The second quarter of 1952 saw production fall generally to 55 per cent of the high levels achieved in 1950 and 1951. Many mills, probably Kirkham & Mannock amongst them, went on to short time working. 65,000 operatives left the industry in nine months and the labour force fell to 82 per cent of its peak post-war level.

In late 1952 there was a recovery. Orders from home and export customers sharply increased. But the sharp reduction in the labour force meant that there was a shortage of workers. The subsequent increase in delivery times did not bode well and allowed overseas competitors an advantage. Lancashire was also slow to modernise and only did so with a feeling of apprehension as to what lay ahead. This at a time when the top marginal rate of income tax had reached 97.5 per cent.

The advent of the Coronation Year of 1953 did not lift the gloom. The price of American cotton was up by 30 per cent. There was a glut of rayon fabrics. The Australian government banned imports and cotton goods therefore were not so much in demand. Banks started to press for a reduction in overdrafts; this was not of immediate concern to Kirkham & Mannock Limited as they had always maintained a prudent balance sheet. It meant however that competitors were dumping stocks of spun cotton at cost, or less, to raise cash.

Isaac and Jack, now in their fifties, were tired of the industry. They had sufficient money not to have the hassle of running what was an increasingly difficult business. It is noticeable that little was spent on buildings, plant or machinery during the four years to December 1952 and indeed thereafter.

The Cotton Spinners' and Manufacturers' Year Book of 1954, apart from drawing attention to the shortage of labour, particularly of young people, listed all the new rules and regulations affecting the industry.

Safety, health and welfare, restrictions on employment of foreign labour, conditions being imposed by fire offices, tax on the importation of foreign machinery whilst the industry was being urged to modernise, a Census of production, demands for increased wages, restrictions on the type of oil to be used on cotton machinery, medical examinations for operatives, keeping of health registers, training allowances and vaccination against variola (smallpox) which could be caught from imported raw cotton, all these rules and regulations had to be taken on board alongside the day to day running of the business.

Whilst the Holdens could accept change for the good of the workers, the plethora of rules and regulations made them question whether or not they wished to continue. To modernise sufficiently would require large capital investment. Should they risk their own personal fortunes by investing in what was an increasingly volatile industry? Isaac, after all, did not have a son to take his place, and had left Oldham some time ago. Jack and Kitty had also left and were also living in Windermere, but with a rural but smart retreat at Mottram St Andrew, some 18 miles south of Manchester.

Kitty was apparently increasingly 'taking to the bottle' and Jack, by now a very large man of some twenty stone, was spending a great deal of time perfecting his large model railway. A talented engineer, he built most of it himself.

It was against this rather unpromising background that Jack's son, John Vernon Holden was brought into the mills. He was a Holden of the fourth generation (founder Ralph, grandfather John and his own father, Jack). His entry gives us the opportunity to look at some other members of the family. This merits another chapter.

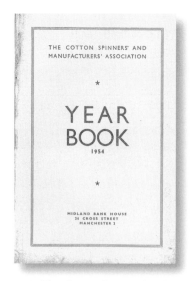

49. The Cotton Spinners' and Manufacturers' Association Year Book 1954 (front cover)

CHAPTER TEN

Ralph Holden's other children

R ALPH HOLDEN HAD DIED in 1916. His widow Alice Green Holden (née Mannock) died in 1924. Five children survived them, four others having died.

We have already seen that John took over the running of the business of Kirkham & Mannock and Prockter & Co. whilst Robert ('Uncle Bob') largely stayed at home but helped to run Simeon Holden Limited with his brother William Mannock Holden ('Uncle Willie').

We have dealt with John's untimely death in 1933 and Uncle Bob's in 1946, but what of the other three?

1. Alice Maud Holden

Alice Maud was born in 1879 and married James Arthur Mellodew in 1905. This was a good match, for the Mellodews owned the well-respected cotton spinning and velvet manufacturing business of Thomas Mellodew & Co. Limited operating at Moorside and Parkfield Mills, Moorside, Oldham. They employed something in the order of 1,000 workers so were a decent-sized concern.

James Arthur's grandfather had been Mayor of Oldham (1875) and his father had died in 1902. James Arthur was employed in the family firm. The prospects should have been favourable!

Although married life started in Oldham itself, it was not long before the couple moved to one of the Mellodew houses at Ripponden Road, Moorside.

Four children were born; Thomas (who died in 1908), Alice born in 1909 who subsequently became Alice Ramage, dying aged 102 in 2012, Alan Percy born in 1911 who died in 1996 and Nancy May who subsequently became Nancy Royce, dying in 2006 aged 93.

James Arthur Mellodew, Alice's husband, was a big dominating man with

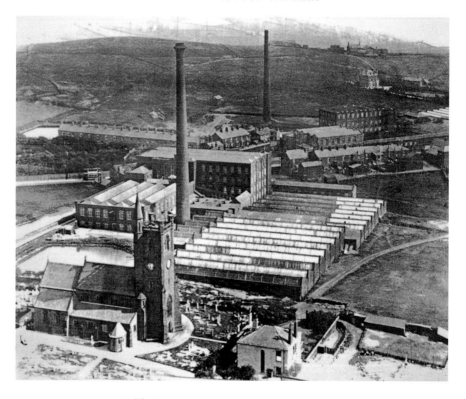

50. The Mellodew Mills at Moorside, Oldham

a presence and, later, with a capacity for drink to match. He was a proficient cricketer playing for the Lancashire Second XI in the Minor Counties Championship. He appears to have been a competent businessman but his bombastic nature alienated him from other members of the Mellodew family.

Alice, by contrast, appears to have been somewhat retiring, preferring to paint rather than manage the household. It is thought that she spent little time with her children and certainly never held a duster! She was all too happy when the family removed from Moorside to the more salubrious environs of South Manchester and settled at Overdale, Bradgate Road, Dunham Massey. Indoor staff and a chauffeur were helpful.

All this was made possible by the income she received from her father's estate later augmented when her mother died in 1924. Her private income in 1926 was £945 from investments (largely her shares in Kirkham & Mannock) and £1,956 from the two trust funds established by her father and mother. Added to James Arthur's income, the couple had a joint income of £6,328 – very comfortable and equating approximately to £253,123 per annum today.

John Holden and James Arthur Mellodew were both businessmen running

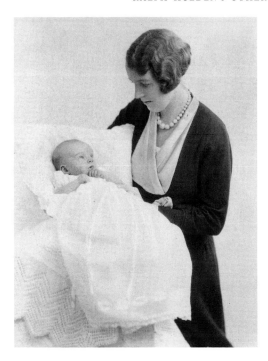

51. Alice Maud Mellodew (née Holden) with Alan Percy Mellodew (1911)

a cotton business. As such they would have had much in common to discuss but there is little evidence that they had much to do with each other.

Family contact was however maintained for appropriate occasions. Indeed when Alan Mellodew married in 1944 cheques came from all members of the Holden family as Alan's account book meticulously recorded.

The Mellodew business suffered from shareholder ructions in 1939/40 and James Arthur resigned. There is no evidence that Alice Maud was at all interested in this. She left it to her daughter Alice Ramage to do all the letter writing and keep the household accounts. Thomas Mellodew & Co. Limited was sold in 1947.

James Arthur Mellodew died in December 1954, a disappointed man as he had expected to die a rich man. His widow stayed on at Overdale. Alice Ramage saw to the staff and the running of the house even though she was now married and living near Macclesfield. Her mother died in a Buxton nursing home in December 1963 without leaving a will – why bother?! She had had a very comfortable life well cushioned by Holden money.

52. Overdale, Bradgate Road, Dunham Massey, Altrincham (home of Mr and Mrs James Arthur Mellodew from 1924)

2. Gertrude

Auntie Gertie as she was known in the family, whatever their generation, left home to marry Dr Robert Peel Parker, son of Mr Samuel Parker of Lostock Hall, Preston in the first quarter of 1911. Like her sister Alice, this too was regarded as a good match.

Dr Parker was a medical practitioner and Superintendent Medical Officer of Health for Oldham. He and Gertie lived in a very nice detached house in Tandle Hill Road, Royton, regarded as a very good address a few miles from Oldham.

His obituary records that 'he had a large private practice and for a good number of years he had been police surgeon at Royton'. This was of course at a time before the National Health Service. His wife's connections would undoubtedly have helped to attract patients. So too would her income have been useful for like Alice she had income from the two Holden trusts as well as income from her Kirkham & Mannock shares. Dr Parker, who was some eight years older than Gertie, died in 1941 aged 63, having retired from practice in 1935.

As for Auntie Gertie, all agreed that in contrast to her sister, she was great fun. She even made light of the burglary that happened whilst she was away. The burglar had not only broken in but made himself at home for some days, using a bed, the bath and the ample supplies in the larder, 'but he'd cleaned the cooker'!

Dr and Mrs Parker had no children. Because she outlived her siblings and did not die until 1968, we will come back to Auntie Gertie again later.

3. William Mannock Holden

Uncle Willie, the youngest child of Ralph and Alice Holden, also married well. His match with Alice Mary (known as May) Gartside connected him to the influential Gartside family who owned the Shiloh Mills at Royton.

The Gartsides were huge employers and immensely successful. Their position is summarised in Duncan Gurr's book on *The Cotton Mills of Oldham*, which sets out the achievements of Thomas Edmund Gartside (1857–1941). Their business was to continue well in to the 1980s.

Shiloh Spinners Limited was a big business. It had a fully paid and issued share capital of £1 million in 1954. This compares with Thomas Mellodew & Co. Limited who had an issued share capital of £107,284 and the £40,000 issued share capital of Kirkham & Mannock Limited. For the year to 3 April

53. Shiloh Mills, Royton

1954 Shiloh showed a profit of £100,955. May would doubtless have benefitted from the dividend declared.

It is said that May Holden was rather timid and her daughter, Joan, likewise. Joan, an only child, was educated at Harrogate Ladies College (as were her cousins Alice and Nancy Mellodew) but unlike her gregarious cousins, she did not enjoy mixing with others.

It is not known what Uncle Willie did –'not very much' according to one member of the family. He was a non-executive director of Shiloh Spinners Limited probably by reason of his wife's connection with the controlling family. Along with his brother Uncle Bob he appears to have helped run the cotton waste business of Simeon Holden but the suggestion is that that was more a 'place to go to' rather than anything else.

He, like his brother and sisters, had money from his parents and dividends from Kirkham & Mannock. Doubtless his wife had money too. They seem to have lived quietly on Windsor Road, Oldham, alongside the other Holdens.

During the Second World War daughter Joan joined the Red Cross. She later declared that it was the only time that she had ever been happy because it gave her a purpose in life.

Following Uncle Bob's death, and the ending of the war, Willie and May

Holden accompanied by unmarried Joan, left Oldham and settled on the
North Wales coast.

Uncle Willie died on 9 April 1956, aged 66, and his wife two days later,
also aged 66. Both died of cancer. It must have been a very unhappy time
for Joan who registered both deaths in Colwyn Bay. A joint funeral service
was held for both parents at Royton Parish Church.

Her grief was unlikely to have been lessened by the death duties payable on
her respective parents' estates. Her father left an estate of £48,594 incurring
estate duty of £15,058. Her mother's estate was £69,806 incurring estate duty
of £35,037 – a reminder of the heavy rate of estate taxes at the time!

These Holdens, by dint of Ralph Holden's fortune, and Prockter money
too, and with the assistance of satisfactory marriages, had managed to enjoy
a comfortable but unostentatious lifestyle for three decades. They would have
been conscious though that they had richer, more successful cousins, and it
is to them that we shall briefly turn to next before dealing with the demise
of Kirkham & Mannock.

54. Miss Joan Holden in
Nurse's uniform

CHAPTER ELEVEN

An overlooked family connection

W E HAVE SEEN THAT Isaac Prockter had a brother, Thomas, who died at the early age of 46 in 1880.

His two daughters who concern us were teenagers at the time. Their subsequent upbringing was doubtless shared between James Prockter, running the Buckley & Prockter department store, Isaac Prockter running Vale Mill and granny Prockter (Bartholomew's widow) living in Chadderton.

Thomas would have been immensely pleased, had he lived, to see his daughter Helena marry William Smith Stott in 1891 at St Margaret's, Hollinwood, and his daughter Lucy Houghton Prockter marry William's brother, Albert Cooper Stott in 1893. Both these Stotts were sons of James Stott.

The importance of the marriages of his nieces into the Stott family would not have been lost on Isaac Prockter and would also, no doubt, have allowed his more ambitious brother-in-law Ralph Holden to claim connection. For, by 1891 James Stott had become important in Oldham circles, as a very successful cotton spinner.

Tradition has it that James Stott was born on 29 December 1837 and was illegitimate. He was thus somewhat younger than William Mannock and the founding Mellodew brothers Thomas and James Mellodew, but they all appear to have started up in the same way renting space in someone else's mill to get their business established.

James Stott made his first deposit of £5 with the Industrial Co-Operative Society of King Street and Werneth, Oldham on 25 October 1860. By 1864 he was renting space at Providence Mill. Duncan Gurr describes this as being occupied by a number of firms. In that year Platt Brothers received an order to manufacture and deliver doubling frames to the mill for James Stott. Similar orders were given in 1865 and 1866. These would have been to James Stott's own specification, one of the cornerstones of his subsequent success.

In old age, Mr Stott was asked how he had managed to do so well. His response was quite simple – 'it was fear of falling down that kept me up'.

But it was also recognised that one of the keys to the success of the Stott business was consideration for the welfare of its employees. By the 1920s for instance they had their own rest and recuperation centre for employees in North Wales. Early on they had their own canteen and, later, a full time State Registered Nurse on the mill premises with a doctor calling in once or twice a week. This was somewhat ahead of their competitors. In addition, there was careful attention to training. This continued throughout the firm's history.

By 1876, Ralph Holden had married Alice Green Mannock and was engaged in his father in law's business of Kirkham & Mannock, and James Stott was sufficiently prosperous to build Coldhurst Hall Mill on Magdela Street, Oldham. This was extended in 1884 and 1892 with an office block being added in 1886. The mill had a modest spindleage of 25,000 in 1889 by which time sons William Smith Stott (then aged 24) and Albert Cooper Stott (then aged 22) were in the mill.

James Stott was not to die until 1919, some three years after Ralph Holden and Isaac Prockter. Unlike them, he was not tempted into local politics. Most detail about his life comes from the memoirs of one Fred Day, who was taken on as an office boy in 1889 at Coldhurst Hall Mill, rising to be manager of both Coldhurst Hall and Werneth Mills.

INTRODUCTION.

———

This pamphlet has been issued with the object of bringing to your attention the progress which has been made during the last few years, in the Cotton Industry and particularly in our own Mills.

There is a First Aid Room at each Mill, with a full time State Registered Nurse in constant attendance, under the supervision of a Doctor who visits each Mill twice weekly; he also examines all New Juveniles.

Boys and girls up to the age of 21 are allowed to have National Milk Cocoa in the morning. A hot midday meal is served in the Canteen at a small cost and during the afternoon, refreshments are sold in the work rooms for a few coppers.

We have modern mechanical transportation to obviate heavy lifting, and are continuously making improvements in the working conditions such as the addition of special Ventilation and Dust Removal Apparatus, Cloak rooms, Washrooms and Lavatories.

Hours of employment are: Monday to Friday from 7-45 a.m. to 5-30 p.m. and Saturday 7-45 a.m. to 12-0 noon with a reduction of four hours per week for Juveniles. The wages paid compare favourably with those of other industries and a Holidays With Pay Scheme, calculated on 4 per cent of gross earnings, is in operation.

For boys and girls employed in the Mills who wish to take advantage of night classes and Technical School, the firm is prepared to pay the fees incurred, and offers the opportunity of attending one afternoon each week at the Technical School, with full pay.

The Cotton Industry played a vital part during the war years, and will still be needed to play a vital part in the peace years, therefore if you are interested in a skilled, useful, and well paid job, now is the opportunity to do something about it.

55. James Stott Limited.
Conditions of Work
(undated)

56. Coldhurst Hall Mill, Magdela Street, Oldham

It was said of James Stott that he was 'shrewd, energetic and conscientious', that he was 'quick to detect faults in machinery' and always on the look out for ways to improve and make cost savings. He was also not afraid to speak his mind.

The memoirs give details of James Stott's preparedness and attention to detail – stockpiling 500 tons of coal in expectation of the miners' strike in 1890, personally inspecting daily the clocking in sheets of the mill employees, checking current fashions and adapting his machinery to spin the yarn those fashions required, and in particular being able to deal efficiently and economically with Indian cotton.

These cottons, sometimes referred to as 'the hindu' had a reputation of being shorter in staple than the Mississippi cottons and dirtier than those of Egypt. In consequence they broke more easily during the spinning process. The hands did not like them for a breakage meant downtime during which, being on piecework, they would not be paid. But, such cottons were cheaper than Egyptian and American cotton.

James Stott recognised that if he could utilise this cheaper cotton he would make a lot of money. He calculated that if he could refine his cotton spinning machinery sufficiently he might avoid the breakages that might otherwise occur in using Indian cotton. He therefore designed and had machinery made to his own detailed specification ('he originated and introduced an extra head making 3 in the drawing frame'), and he changed the conventional doubling frame.

Further he was ruthless in seeing to the cleaning of his machinery, recognising that he was spinning inferior cotton which might be dirty. Unusually in a spinning mill, he had his machinery stopped at set intervals for cleaning purposes. Most of his fellow spinners would run their machines as long as possible, usually until there was a break.

At very little cost therefore he improved the quality of the yarn produced and this gave him a price advantage as compared with other spinners.

Specialising in Indian cotton meant a natural progression into manufacturing carpet yarn. Previously the yarn required by carpet manufacturers had to be dyed before delivery as the manufacturers would not accept white yarn. To obviate the necessity of dyeing, Mr Stott sought out natural coloured cotton; this he got from India, known as coconade. This is a tangerine colour, was cheaper than a dyed yarn and was an instant success.

In the main, through invention and adjustment, the James Stott firm began to be known for spinning coarse counts of yarn suitable for carpets, canvas and the like. It was acknowledged that James Stott was at the forefront of doubling frame improvements.

His growth was similar to that of the Mellodews some decades earlier who had recognised that they had to adapt their looms to produce the high quality cotton velvets for which they became well known. They carefully patented all their inventions. Mellodews continued to invent and were still applying for new patents as late as 1933.

In contrast, the Holdens at Kirkham & Mannock seemed content to pursue a steady path as traditional cotton spinners and doublers. There is little evidence of further extension to their mills after 1890, nor any experimentation with cotton spinning machinery.

Increasing years – and he was now in his fifties – did not stop Mr Stott from speaking his mind. Some 30 years after starting in business Mr Stott perchanced in the Bath Hotel to meet a Mr Percival, who had troubled him greatly in the past. The beaming Mr Percival advanced, hand outstretched, to meet the respected cotton spinner. The latter, instead of accepting the proffered handshake, led him to a large looking glass over the mantelpiece and said 'Just look through there and you will see a damned waistrel'. Mr Percival was not sure to whom the reference was directed as a look in the mirror showed all those who were present, including himself. The point was made.

Similar remarks were made to those who failed to settle their accounts on time. Mr Stott regarded this as a personal affront and took the view that 'if they couldn't pay one week, they cannot pay two'.

His son William, who dealt with sales, had been doing business quite successfully with a Romanian firm of shippers, based in Manchester. They had started to fall behind with their payments. William found that whenever he called on the principal, he had 'just gone out' and they 'did not know when he might return'. With some reluctance, William reported the matter to his father.

Mr Stott, by now reaching retirement age, felt quite equal to dealing with the situation. He warmly wrapped himself up in old clothes, armed himself with newspapers and sandwiches and called on the principal who 'had just gone out' and they 'did not know when he would be back'. Mr Stott settled himself to wait on the bench outside the principal's office. He enjoyed his newspapers and his sandwiches. He had not long to wait before his quarry emerged ready to go out for lunch. Evidently he had been in his office all along. Straight talking took place and Mr Stott departed with a cheque, banking the same immediately. A few years later, payments again fell behind. Mr William told the customer that he would arrange for his father to call. Hastily the customer said 'No, don't send that old man again', and paid up.

Mr Stott did not like to be taken advantage of. There is the amusing tale of him giving a lift in his carriage to a fellow director of Bank Top Spinning Co. Limited. James Stott had ordered his carriage to be stopped when he saw the man waiting in the rain at the tramstop. The following week, as Mr Stott's carriage approached the same tram stop, the gentleman concerned stepped into the road, the coachman stopped the carriage and the pedestrian got in. Later, Mr Stott enquired of his coachman if this fellow director had given him anything. The answer being in the negative, next week when the man stepped into the road expecting the carriage to stop, Mr Stott in a loud voice instructed his coachman to 'drive on'.

As his business grew, so did his status and it was not surprising that Mr Stott was asked to join the board of directors of other Oldham companies. He was, for instance, Chairman of Granville Mill Co. Limited (who by 1915 had a spindleage of 100,000 mules and a 1,000 hp engine) and a director of Ruby Mill Co. Limited (spindleage of 82,000 in 1915 and a 1,200 hp engine).

Caution was a by word so far as James Stott was concerned. Many in Oldham put their savings in to mill loan accounts. They felt happy that they could see where their money was deposited. Mr Stott reminded people that there was no security for their loans.

With money not required for his business, he preferred to purchase property and invest in the purchase of shares in companies such as the Manchester Ship Canal Company and Trafford Park Estates Limited.

His caution extended to those in his own workplace. Whilst happy if an employee wished to leave to better their position, he urged caution. A manager, Mr Linney, was thinking of leaving Mr Stott's employ and going into the cotton waste trade. When he told Mr Stott, he was surprised when the old man said, 'Come with me to The Falstaff!' That public house was a rendezvous and business place for waste dealers. Mr Stott took Mr Linney to the door and they both looked inside. Mr Stott said, 'Now tell me Linney, how many are there here that you would like to trust?' Mr Linney stayed on!

By 1904, the Stotts had outgrown Coldhurst Hall Mill; the earlier extensions had absorbed the extra capacity needed. In addition to increased spinning of coarse yarns, they were increasingly weaving. Further manufacturing capacity was required.

Near at hand on Manchester Road, Oldham was Werneth Mill. The original mill having been burnt down in 1881 and the mill having been largely rebuilt and extended in 1882 to 1883, it was suitable for the Stotts' purpose. James Stott Limited (for that is what the business had now become) purchased it in 1904. The weaving shed adjacent to Manchester Road was partially rebuilt and other extensions took place.

57. Park House, 77 Queen's Road, Oldham (2016) James Stott's home

By the start of the First World War, James Stott was 76 and beginning to feel his age. This did not put him off business. He had got thus far by careful attention to his business, an ability to improve his machinery, an established training system for his employees and a concentration on spinning the yarn needed for the manufacture of canvas and similar goods.

Four of his five sons, all now in their 40s were in the business and grandsons were beginning to shape up too.

Unfortunately, like the Mellodews, tragedy struck in the war. A grandson, Lieutenant James Stott, was killed at Gallipoli in 1915. The family provided the James Stott Memorial Chapel at St John's Church, Werneth, Oldham (deconsecrated in 1983).

When he died on 20 June 1919 at his home Park House, 77 Queens Road, Oldham (a very good address opposite Alexandra Park) James Stott left the substantial estate of £254,489. This was a huge sum, roughly equivalent to £10 million today. It shows how successful he had been as a businessman.

Provision was made for his surviving four daughters. A fund of £16,000 was set up for each of them from which they were to receive the income; the capital to go to their children.

His wife was provided for by the gift of Park House, its contents and an annuity of £1,500 per annum (giving her not less than the equivalent of £60,000 pa today). This was a handsome amount but alas she was not long to enjoy it as she died within six months of her husband on 21 January 1920. She left Park House and its contents to her unmarried son Ernest and unmarried daughter Gertrude.

The residue of James Stott's estate went to his four sons William Smith Stott (married to Helena Prockter), Albert Cooper Stott (married to Lucy Houghton Prockter), Harry Stott and Ernest Stott. In effect they inherited the business of James Stott Limited, which had been incorporated on 18 April 1893 with a share capital of £80,000.

The Holdens no doubt watched on with interest, but as their own mills were doing well as a result of war, there was no need for jealousy. All they could do is congratulate their cousins on their good fortune.

In the two decades that followed, whilst Kirkham & Mannock and Prockter & Co. plodded on making a decent enough living for their owners and paying dividends, James Stott Limited continued to invest and expand.

Coldhurst Hall Mill was extended in 1919 and 1920. Werneth Mill added a new weaving shed and a three storey extension in 1924.

By the 1930s, when most Oldham spinning companies were facing financial difficulties (see ante p. 51), Stott's was sufficiently confident to take

LOYAL OLDHAM LINES ROYAL ROUTE

AFTER spending the night in the Royal train at a quiet siding at Turton, between Bolton and Bury, the Queen today continued her Lancashire tour to meet men and women in the cotton industry's production drive. Her Majesty first visited Blackburn and later lunched with the Mayor and Mayoress of Rochdale and prominent citizens at Rochdale Town Hall, leaving for her visits to Oldham and Ashton at 1 45 p.m.

The Queen entered Oldham from Royton soon after two o'clock, and all along the Rochdale Road route cheering schoolchildren and townspeople occupied every available open space and vantage point

Outside works, mills and business premises employees waited in the rain to watch Her Majesty pass. Housewives had left their shopping and home duties, loyal householders and shopkeepers had decorated their homes and premises, and Union Jacks were flown from buildings along the processional route.

Gaily Festooned

Magdala Street and the entrance to the Coldhurst Hall Mill were festooned with gay pennants and bunting for the occasion, and there the wave of excitement and enthusiasm reached its height as the Queen's car, the second in a procession of eight or nine, rounded the bend and drew up at the mill gates.

Mr. Harold Wilson, President of the Board of Trade, and Mr. George Isaacs, Minister of Labour, met the Queen at Blackburn Station and accompanied her throughout the tour.

Because of the heavy rain the Director of Education (Mr. M. Harrison) decided to cancel the buses which were to have transported the Oldham children to positions on the processional route, but this apparently made little difference, and they lined the route in their thousands. Headmasters of schools in the vicinity of the route had been mitted to use their discreti

By one o'clock crowds were lining the roads at Royton, and everyone was in happy mood, cheering on every vehicle that passed, from push bikes to milk floats.

Royton Town Hall was gaily decorated with flags and bunting, and the Chairman (Councillor Fred Ford) and members of the Council paid the official tribute from the steps as the Royal procession drove by.

At Coldhurst Hall Mill

All along Rochdale Road the crowds roared a welcome and at 2 20 the Royal car drew up at a platform erected in the Coldhurst Hall Mill yard.

The Queen stepped from her car to be introduced to the Mayor (Councillor S. Thornton) by Earl Peel, Lord Lieutenant of Lancashire, and, after chatting for a few moments with the Town Clerk and the Chief Constable she was taken up in the hoist to the winding room.

Some of the crowds, mostly composed of women, had been waiting since shortly after noon to see Her Majesty.

A quartet of old ladies were cheerfully standing in Magdala Street, oblivious of the weather and singing popular songs played by the British Legion Band. They were 82-year-old Mrs. Mary Coulston, of Rochdale Road, 77-year-old Mrs. Parkinson, of Rochdale Road, Mrs. Stocks (75), of Coldhurst Street, and Mrs. Baguley (76), who had travelled from her home in Fields New Road, Chadderton, to see the Queen. Mrs. Coulston said, "We don't care about the weather, we

58. The Queen's visit to Coldhurst Hall Mill (1948) (*OEC* 2 June 1948)

over the Hartford Mill on Block Lane, Oldham. This was a big mill, having a spindleage of 120,000 in 1915. The mill had been erected in 1907 and extended in 1919 and 1924.

The final purchase by James Stott Limited was in 1947 when the company bought Pine Mill on Sherwood Street. This building had been built in 1890 and extended in 1902 and 1940 and later in 1942 when it was being used as an aircraft munitions factory. One suspects that given the end of the war and reduction in munition manufacture, Stott's may have been able to acquire this mill 'on the cheap'.

This continued expansion throughout the 1920s, '30s and '40s showed the Stotts' confidence in their ability to make money. Of course, their business profited from government work received in the Second World War. Not only was there a great demand for canvas but Stott's made water sausages, the containers towed by ship to transport water to places where it was otherwise in short supply.

The Mellodews sold out to Balstone Cooke and Rayonese Limited in 1947. There had been no obvious successor to carry their firm on. It was recognised that Alan Mellodew was not up to it; in any event there were quarrelling shareholders. The family was glad to be out of the business.

The two Holdens, Isaac and Jack, had left Oldham and it was becoming clear that Jack's son, John Vernon Holden, was probably not going to be equipped to carry on the business of Kirkham & Mannock. In any event there had been little investment in updating machinery. Prockter & Co. had of course ceased.

In contrast, James Stott Limited thrust ahead. The firm well exceeded the targets set by Sir Stafford Cripps in 1948 for productivity. The importance of the firm was recognised by Coldhurst Hall Mill being included in the Queen's itinerary when on her 1948 Lancashire tour.

Re-organisation at Hartford Mill resulted in a 12 per cent decrease in the wage bill and increased productivity. A joint venture was explored with the then huge firm of Turner & Newall, who made brake linings. Urwick Orr and Partners Limited, specialists in organisation and management, were instructed to review the firm. Their report cost £16,655 but identified savings of about £17,815 per annum. So, the Stotts did not stand still. They even advertised, something unheard of by the likes of Kirkham & Mannock who viewed it as a waste of resources.

But even the Stotts had to think about the future. William Smith Stott, James Stott's eldest son, died in October 1951, having outlived his younger brothers. He left a satisfactory estate of £111,000 although it was surprising that it was not more. The size elicited the comment that 'he had done very well' not in leaving so much but in having managed to give so much away to lessen the amount of estate duty! His sons, Prockter Stott and Albert Houghton Stott were now running the firm along with Harry's son, Alan. Like the Mellodews, the firm was being run by cousins. Prockter Stott was to die in 1953, aged 58, and Albert was coming up to 60.

It was no surprise therefore that when an offer was made on 7 October 1955 by their friendly competitor John Bright and Brothers Limited of Rochdale, such offer was accepted. And it was a good offer – 800,000 ordinary shares in John Bright's and £1,000,000 in cash. The *Oldham Chronicle*, in reporting the sale, showed how big Stott's had become. They had 1,400 employees and they had been stunningly profitable.

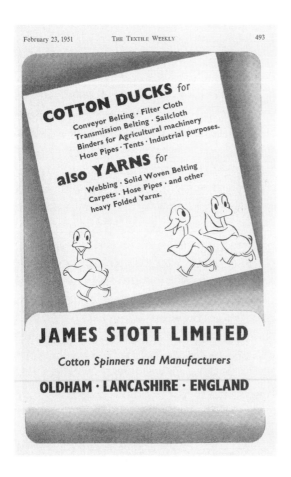

59. James Stott Limited advertisement. (Textile Weekly. February 1951)

The pre-tax profits for the firm for the last three years had averaged about £285,000 with satisfactory profits anticipated for the takeover year. Furthermore the Stotts had been very conservative; they had recognised that mill property in Oldham was virtually unsaleable and had written down their fixed assets – the mills – to nil. Their balance sheet still showed assets of just under £1.4 million.

Bright's made canvas and cord fabric for tyres. They reckoned that Stott's high grade canvas and carpet threads would fit in well with their own business.

Completion of the sale took place on 9 November 1955. Two months earlier Thomas Mellodew & Co. Limited had gone into receivership, having been sold in 1947 for £320,000.

As for the Stotts themselves, they had enjoyed their great prosperity. They had lived comfortably on Windsor Road, as had the Holdens. The house Westlands had been divided into two; William Smith Stott and his wife Helena (née Prockter) had occupied one half and brother Albert Cooper Stott and his wife Lucy Houghton (née Prockter) had occupied the other. So, like the Mannocks at 62/64 Napier Street East, two sisters lived next door to each other.

Albert Houghton Stott had married Dora Tweedale (bringing with her what was rumoured to be a substantial dowry) and lived at The Knoll, Windsor Road, a large distinctive property. She was from the family that ran Tweedales and Smalley (1920) Limited of Castleton, Rochdale, a well known firm of textile machinery manufacturers.

After Albert Cooper Stott died in 1924, 'Auntie Lucy' (so called by all generations) was declared to be very rich 'as she had Uncle Albert's money'. She had no children but she had Stott and Prockter money. Her uncle James Prockter had left her £5,000 when he died in 1916 and income from 2/24th of his estate. She had also benefitted from the estate of her father, Thomas Prockter. Albert Cooper Stott left an estate valued at £151,641. With her second husband, Mr R. T. Whitaker (who may have had money too!?) she moved to Birkdale, near Southport. She determined to enjoy life and apparently had a Rolls Royce, a uniformed chauffeur and two maids.

She proffered advice to her family – 'be good, but if you can't be good, be careful, and if you can't be careful, buy a pram'. She was rumoured to have had several fur coats, a different one for each day of the week. She died in 1941 leaving an estate of £54,000 which suggests that she had made inroads into her capital to fund her lifestyle. Mr Whitaker survived her taking up residence at The Prince of Wales Hotel, Southport, until his death in 1949. Lucy's sister Helena living then at Lytham St Annes had died in 1940.

When Auntie Lucy left Westlands for Birkdale, her house was taken over by Lord Emmott, the same Lord Emmott that we met earlier. He was to die suddenly in February 1926. His barony became extinct on his death as he had no male issue.

After the sale to Bright's, the remaining Stotts left Oldham, Albert and Dora retiring to Jersey. Only the Holdens, of what will have appeared to be a large interwoven family, retained a business there. This is the subject of our next chapter.

James Stott's 4 mills to be sold in £1m deal

TWO old-established family concerns, one in Oldham and the other in Rochdale, are involved in one of the biggest mill deals for some time, in which 800,000 shares and a cash payment of £1 million will change hands. The firms concerned are James Stott, Ltd., who own four mills in Oldham, and John Bright and Sons, Ltd., who have mills at Rochdale.

It is announced by Mr. E. P. Andreae (chairman of John Bright's) that an agreement has been entered into whereby the company will acquire the whole of the issued capital of James Stott Ltd. The consideration for the purchase is to be satisfied by the issue, credited as fully paid to the shareholders of James Stott, of 800,000 of the unissued ordinary shares of 5s. each in the capital of John Bright's, and a cash payment of £1 million. The acquisition will be effected on November 9.

"James Stott Ltd. was originally founded in 1861. and has continued as a privately-owned concern to enjoy a very high reputation" it is stated. "In more recent years the scope of the business has been considerably extended. The freehold and long leasehold land and buildings include four mills, namely the Coldhurst Hall, Werneth, Hartford and Pine Mills, all in Oldham and within easy reacch of one another. Apart from spinning and doubling sections James Stott has for many years past specialised in the manufacture of the highest-grade canvas cloths, and in this field, in weight of output its business is second only to that of John Bright and Sons, Ltd.

Trading profit

It is further pointed out that trading profits of James Stott Ltd., for the last three financial periods ended December 15, have been £294,918 in 1952, £270,135 in 1953, and £296,582 in 1954. It was anticipated that the results for the current period ending in December will be satisfactory, although they will show, to some extent, the effect of falling profit margins generally experienced today.

60. Announcement of the takeover of James Stott Limited (*OEC* 7 October 1955)

CHAPTER TWELVE

The end of the Firm

B Y 1955 WITH ISAAC HOLDEN and Jack both living in the Lake District and, in effect, retired, although only aged 57 and 52 respectively, the future of Kirkham & Mannock became a pressing family problem.

Isaac and Jack had really lost interest. Both were sufficiently well placed financially not to need to rely on Kirkham & Mannock for their living, although the directors' fees and dividends were useful.

Isaac had one daughter, Barbara, now married to architect Hugh Brady. Jack had two children, John Vernon Holden (born 1931) and Rosemary (born 1935).

So if the business were to continue under the day to day control of the family, it would have to be run by John Vernon Holden, assisted by managers. To give these managers status, the company's articles of association were altered in 1955. These created a new post of 'Official Director'. This would enable significant employees once appointed to call themselves a director, which would give them credibility so far as outsiders were concerned.

Such a position would not appear to give the individuals any real power as the articles made it quite clear that they were not to be entitled to have access to the books of the company nor to attend directors' meetings!

John Vernon Holden was wholly unsuited to run the business of Kirkham & Mannock. He had been educated at Rugby School and been sent to study accountancy, which he disliked. It was sport that really interested him. He had been spoilt.

As a child, the household had a nanny, maids and a chauffeur. He used to be taken by the chauffeur to school. His father had made most decisions for him, one of which was that he should go in to the mills.

John was tall, blond and good looking. It didn't help that his marriage to the glamorous Shelagh Doughty in 1956 was perhaps not what his parents Jack and Kitty would have hoped for.

61. A family outing – Jack and Kitty Holden, Mrs Isaac Holden and young John
Vernon Holden holding 'the catch'

Her family background was acceptable. Her father was in the textile trade
as a merchant converter and the family had clothing connections. But, they
were obviously not as well-heeled as the Holdens.

Shelagh had won a scholarship to what is now Cheadle Hulme School, a
prestigious school, but without the snob value of Harrogate Ladies College!

Shelagh was a strong character, a model with assignments from *Elle*, *Vogue*
and other prestigious organisations.

Jack and Kitty were perhaps wary of a talented daughter-in-law. Jack was
reluctant to let her know anything about the business and any correspondence
(whether business or not) was sent to John at the mills, not the matrimonial
home.

Shelagh recalls that on her first introduction to the Marsland Mills she was
confronted by a sign which said 'strippers and grinders' wanted. The modelling
world is very broad minded but this sign was not what Shelagh expected to
see on an Oldham cotton mill. It was explained to her that a stripper and
grinder was one who maintained machinery in a cotton mill, specifically a
worker who removed detritus from a carding machine.

In reality, Shelagh might have made a better job of running the mills

62. Wedding of John Vernon Holden to Shelagh Doughty (1956)

than her husband, but really the writing was on the wall for this size and type of business.

The accounts of Kirkham & Mannock (Holdings) Limited (of which Kirkham & Mannock Limited had become a subsidiary) for the year ended 5 April 1957 showed a reassuring position. The company (and its subsidiary) had made a trading profit of £7,689 (up from £4,967 the previous year), had investment and bank interest income of £1,981, had cash in the bank (rather than an overdraft), plentiful reserves and proposed to pay a final dividend to its shareholders of £3,000 on top of its interim payment of the same amount (both the same as the previous year).

But it was clear that the business was running down. Its stock was reduced by 18 per cent to £97,000 and its debtors were down by over 43 per cent, indicating a much reduced level of trading. This accounted for the satisfactory 'cash at bank' position of over £53,000. The company also held buildings, plant and machinery which were in the accounts at £34,000 (after depreciation).

Even if John Holden had been capable of running the business, to keep it going would require a large investment in new machinery so as to keep

Money is such a vulgar necessity

63. Shelagh Doughty,
later Mrs John Vernon
Holden (1956), modelling
(on the left)

the firm competitive. John didn't really want to run the business and whilst his father and uncle were alive would probably not have been given a free hand to do so.

The business was solvent, but its future was uncertain. Fortunately, it was not long before the government came to the Holdens' rescue.

Like 1955 before it, 1959 was a year of severe recession throughout the industry with extensive short-time working, which had started in August 1958.

The year also saw the end of the Yarn Spinners' Association Agreement, a scheme for controlling yarn prices, which was formed after the war in 1946 and continued uninterrupted until ended by the Restrictive Practices Court, after lengthy court proceedings. In reality it had probably come to an end anyway as spinning companies had been dumping yarn at cost to raise cash. Still, while it lasted, the Agreement had provided a comfortable cushion on price.

Throughout the nineteenth century the British cotton industry had satisfied a large proportion of the world demand for cotton goods. In 1912 it still accounted for two-thirds of the international trade in cotton goods, when it exported 6,900 million yards out of a production of 8,050 million yards. Between 1912 and 1958, annual production of cotton fabrics fell by almost 75 per cent (i.e. From 8,050 to 2,000 million yards) largely because of the decline in exports from 6,900 million yards to 450 million yards. Imports increased considerably so that by 1958 the United Kingdom was a net importer of cotton fabrics.

The fall in demand for British cotton textile goods was accompanied by a marked reduction in machinery installed. Companies were dependent on what had become old fashioned machinery.

The difficulties of declining sales and old plant were aggravated by structural defects in the industry. Its horizontal structure, which divided the various manufacturing stages (spinning, doubling, weaving, finishing and converting) into separate compartments suitable for a large and varied world market, had become a source of weakness. This was not helped by the multiplicity of small firms.

The conclusion of voluntary agreements between the British cotton industry and the cotton industries of India, Pakistan and Hong Kong, limiting imports of low-priced cotton goods, provided a particularly favourable opportunity for a complete overhaul of the industry.

Discussions took place between representatives of the industry and government. The result was the Cotton Industry Act, 1959.

There were to be two types of aid to the industry. There was to be compensation for the elimination of excess capacity by the closure of mills and scrapping of surplus machinery under re-organisation schemes. And, there were to be grants towards the cost of re-equipment and modernisation to those firms who stayed in business and agreed to re-equip.

Under the schemes dealing with excess capacity, the government agreed to pay two-thirds of the compensation for the scrapping of obsolete equipment, the remaining one third to be paid by firms remaining in the industry, spread over a number of years. This became known as 'the scrappage scheme', and it was a condition that the machinery should actually be broken up to avoid it being sold to developing counties, which would only aggravate the problem the government was trying to solve.

A further fund was set up to make provision for redundant operatives. This was the first scheme of its kind and well in advance of state legislation, which was later contained in the Redundancy Payments Act, 1965.

So far as re-equipment was concerned, the Act provided that the government might make grants of up to 25 per cent of the cost of modernising existing machinery and buying and installing new equipment in the five years following the coming in to force of the Act.

It did not take the Holdens long to make up their mind. The scheme was announced in August. Redundancies were announced at the Marsland Mills on 18 September 1959, with the mills to close from 1 January 1960. Isaac and Jack Holden told John that he should look for another job. There had been no consultation with him. The decision was made.

Other firms moved with equal speed. Shiloh Spinners announced the closure of three of their mills, reducing their remaining number to five. By 3 November, 500 firms had applied for compensation from the scrappage scheme. In the general election campaign of a month earlier the Conservative Party Manifesto was able to trumpet that 'reorganisation and re-equipment of the Lancashire Cotton Industry has got away to a good start'.

Potential loss of jobs caused considerable disquiet in Oldham. The MP for Oldham West, Mr Hales, pointed out that he knew of 12 mills in his constituency that would close before Christmas, which could leave 3,000 people out of work. The President of the Board of Trade, Mr Reginald Maudling, when asked in Parliament about this, did not see this as a difficulty; he understood there was a shortage of labour in the cotton industry so redundant operatives would soon be re-employed.

From the operatives' point of view, if they left employment on hearing that their employer might close, and got another job, they forfeited any right to compensation. Whereas, if they stayed and were made redundant, they would get compensation. This was particularly hard on those who had been with the same firm for many years, but who did not wish to risk being unemployed.

It is interesting to peruse the applications from Kirkham & Mannock Limited employees for claims for compensation for loss of employment, or status, or of earnings (because they had had to take a lesser paid job). All these applications are held by John Rylands Library of the University of Manchester (under reference OLD/5/21). They show the wide variety of jobs in each section of the business. In no particular order:

(a)   Cotton Doubling Section – winder, spooler, bobbin carrier, reeler, piecer, beamer, overlooker, doubling major, boiler fireman, oiler and greaser, warehouseman, packer and cleaner.

(b)   Cotton Spinning Section – ring spinner, mule and ring overlooker, card tenter, draw frame tenter, spare tenter, intermediate tenter, head doffer, weft carrier, bobbin carrier, blowing room major, tube sorter, stripper and grinder, spinner piecer, creeler, rover tenter, carder, slubber tenter, mule spinner, ring jobber, head cotton chamber man, ring doffer, stoker, engineer, warehouseman, packer, clerk, nurse, night-watchman, cleaner and lodge keeper.

The wages seemed to vary between £5.65 per week for a ring doffer, £7.45 per week or thereabouts for a ring spinner, £18.55 per week for the engineer and something in between for the others. The Mill Manager, a Mr Thomas Walker, was paid £29.90 per week.

The applications show that the majority of employees had managed to get another job, mostly in the cotton industry, and were mostly aged between 48 and 71 years of age. Many of them had worked for Kirkham & Mannock Limited for several years.

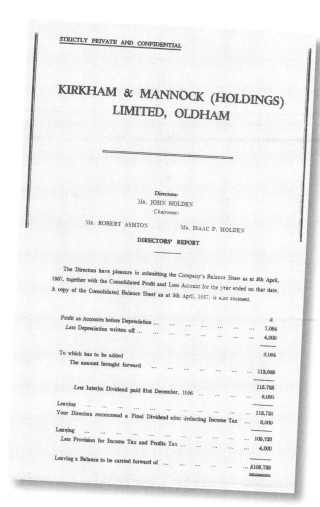

64. Kirkham & Mannock (Holdings) Limited – frontsheet to accounts for year ended 5 April 1957

At this distance in time, it is difficult to gauge what the reaction of John Vernon Holden might have been. He was 28 at the time. Although he had not been academically successful, he might have expected that Kirkham & Mannock Limited would continue to provide him with a comfortable living and that a relaxed lifestyle would continue.

The actual closure decided by his father and his uncle must have come as a shock. According to his claim for compensation, at closure, he was employed as a salesman at the rate of £21.05 per week. He confirmed that he was ill from 2 April until 14 May 1960 and became self-employed thereafter.

It is ironic that almost immediately after the scrappage scheme came into force there was a boom in demand for textile goods throughout the world. By July 1960 Mr Maudling was able to hail the scrappage scheme a success. He confirmed that the estimated cost to date was about £13 million, with the likely cost to be about £30 million. He said 'The fact that the textile trade is now prospering does not seem to me to justify interfering with a scheme that is working well'. Concern was still being expressed at the high proportion of old machinery in use and the inadequacy of shift working arrangements.

However, these were no longer the concern of the directors of Kirkham & Mannock Limited. An orderly realisation of assets was now their priority.

Duncan Gurr tells us that after 1959, the No. 1 Mill was in multi-occupation until demolition in 1990, No. 2 was similarly used until demolition in 1991. Both sites have now been redeveloped for commercial purposes.

CHAPTER THIRTEEN

Postscript

ALTHOUGH THE BUSINESS OF Kirkham & Mannock Limited had gone, one is always curious to know what became of those previously so concerned with it.

Alice Mellodew had died in December 1963 and Auntie Gertie Parker, the last survivor of Ralph Holden's children, died on 26 May 1968, aged 83. As mentioned earlier, Robert Parker had died some 21 year before and there were no children.

Auntie Gertie had been interested in the fortunes of Kirkham & Mannock Limited, not only because her father ran it until 1916 and her brother, John Holden until 1933, but because under her father and mother's wills, she was in receipt of income from the company.

Although her brother, Willie, had also left her income from his estate thinking she was poorly provided for, she actually was comfortably placed. Concerned at the likely size of the estate duty bill on her death, she decided to try to outwit the taxman by making gifts and surviving the appropriate period.

Unfortunately, the good reaper called some three and a half years too early. Gifts during her lifetime to her nephews and nieces, and great nephew and nieces, to the value of £101,000 had to be added back into her estate for calculation of estate duty. There was some reduction because of the time that had elapsed, but part of her estate of £334,000 was to suffer tax at 65 per cent and with additional tax because of the gifts made, there was a liability of £239,000. It then transpired that Auntie Gertie's income tax affairs were somewhat in arrears – £36,000 was owed in tax!

This was not good news to the beneficiaries, the three children of Alice Mellodew (Alice Ramage, Nancy Royce and Alan Mellodew), Joan Holden and John Holden's three grandchildren. At the end of the day, Alan Mellodew received £10,050, a considerable disappointment from what at the outset promised to be a good inheritance.

65. A relaxed Isaac Holden

Worse was to follow. On 2 November 1964, Auntie Gertie had released her right to income from the estates of Ralph and Alice Holden, her father and mother. The capital therefore fell back into the other children's estates, all of whom had already died, and was distributed. Because Auntie Gertie had not survived this release by five years, this transaction too became taxable on her death. estate duty was to be paid by the beneficiaries who had received the money. Alan Mellodew, for example, had to find approximately £2,000. Administratively, it meant opening up the other four Holden estates (John, Robert, Alice and Willie). The whole business was not finally settled until 20 November 1974.

Meantime, Gertie's house at Birnam, Tandle Hill Road, Royton was sold for £13,500, her 1963 Rover 650 car for a few hundreds and legacies paid to her doctor and to her chauffeur, Mr Watt.

Of course, the tax bill would have been no less if Auntie Gertie had taken no tax saving measures, but it still must have been galling to have received some money, only to have to pay some back! It illustrates the high tax rates of the time.

Auntie Gertie's estate held only one cotton-spinning company share – Bee Spinning Co. Limited. She also held shares in Oldham Brewery, but otherwise there was little evidence of her connection with Oldham. She was said to have been lively and this might explain why her portfolio included a surprising number of holdings in various tea plantation companies – a lively speculation?! These were sold.

The sales were made on the Oldham Stock Exchange, which was to close in 1975. As an aside, it is interesting to note that, as reported in the

Daily Telegraph on 21 April 2010, the Liberal Democrat party floated the idea of creating a 'network of Regional Stock Exchanges to act as regional platforms, matching local investors with growing small businesses to provide cost effective access to equity'. Nothing came of this suggestion.

The Holdens continued to enjoy themselves. Family weddings were well attended. They were able to watch developments in Oldham with detachment.

Stott's Werneth Mill ceased production under John Bright's ownership in 1960 and the majority of that mill was razed in 1967, leaving some weaving sheds to be redeveloped as a garage and workshop. Mellodew's Parkfield Mill was demolished in 1969 and the site redeveloped for housing. Their Moorside Mill, after partial demolition and shared occupation, was eventually cleared and that site too developed for housing.

Isaac Prockter Holden, the eldest of the third generation, died aged 72 in 1970. He had remained away from Oldham and by the time of his death was living at Bexhill-on-Sea, Sussex. He left a very satisfactory estate of £173,011, which was greatly depleted by estate duty of £97,616 – an overall rate of tax in excess of 50 per cent; a further painful reminder of the high rate of death duties at that time.

66. A family wedding – Hugh Brady, Barbara Brady, Mrs Isaac Holden,
Mrs John Vernon Holden (Shelagh)

100 years at Coldhurst come crashing down

AFTER 100 years of towering over the Coldhurst area, the chimney of the Coldhurst Hall Mill came crashing down on Sunday morning.

The chimney is the last part of the mill to be demolished, after the mill had been the subject of a controversial argument.

A large crowd gathered on Magdala Street to

watch the chimney crumble into the remains of the mill it once served.

Coldhurst Hall closed as a cotton mill in 1971 when the John Bright textile group put the building up for sale.

It was bought by Mr.

Merton Lister, and controversy followed when Mr. Lister applied for planning permission to change part of the factory for commercial use.

Permission was refused, and Mr. Lister was later found dead in the mill.

Pictures: VINCENT BROWN

67. Coldhurst Hall Mill chimney demolition

His younger brother Jack was to die four years later in September 1974 aged 71. He had kept some business connections, putting money into Nadens, who were sheet metal fabricators.

For the last few years of his life he had led what could be viewed as a somewhat unsettled existence.

His wife, Kitty, had become increasingly subject to bouts of depression and it has been suggested that her condition was not helped by a propensity to drink. She was not to die until 1983 aged 77, obsessed by all accounts that she might be short of money, and of course after the death of her only son (see below).

And, she certainly would have missed her daily outings, for she and Jack had taken lunch out every day – no wonder he became such a large man!

The move to Mottram St Andrew had been followed by a move to Tarporley, near Chester, where there was a house with stabling for the benefit of their daughter, Rosemary. Her marriage encouraged a move to Whalley, near Skipton. Rosemary was careful to look after her mother. Jack's relationship with his son was not perhaps as close. Kitty Holden disapproved of her glamorous and formidable daughter-in-law.

The final link of the Holdens with Oldham was broken with the tragic death of Jack's only son, John Vernon Holden, on 2 March 1978, aged 46. For some one of his modest age, he left a very respectable estate of £107,270, including his house in Grasscroft, Oldham.

Kitty did not call to give comfort to her daughter-in-law after John's death. She sent her sister to enquire 'what had happened'.

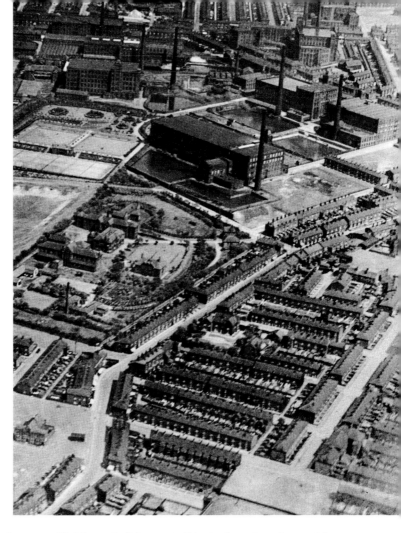

68. Aerial view of part of Oldham, showing the area of Werneth and the Mill landscape 1933 (courtesy OLSA 1979 *The Cotton Mills of Oldham* publication)

After his redundancy at Kirkham & Mannock Limited, and owing to his interest in sport, John had business interests in The 'W' Sportswear Limited (by way of shares and loan capital) manufacturing rugby shirts and shorts. But it was clear that he was no businessman.

He had Oldham interests by way of shares in Oldham Brewery and Joseph Clegg (Holdings) Limited, of which James Arthur Mellodew had been chairman. This company was the holding company of the better known Eli Lees Co. Limited. A reversionary interest, through his mother, in Vernon Heywood Stott's estate, showed his financial connection with that family.

And so, after John Vernon's death, the only related member of the family remaining in Oldham, was Alan Mellodew, living at Moorside. This grandson of Ralph Holden died on 19 February 1996, aged 84. Fortunately he, and other members of the Holden family, had retained some family papers, without which this chronicle could not have been written. Alan had no children and left a respectable estate of £216,706, aided by his several Holden inheritances.

Alan's cousin, Joan Holden, was to die later in 1996, aged 76. She had long since left Oldham, having lived on the North Wales coast at the time of her parents' death and lastly in Southport, near to Formby Golf Club where she had been a keen member.

Like so many prominent cotton families therefore, the Holdens have dispersed and, for them, Oldham and their industrious forebears in the cotton industry are a matter of history. The landscape of the town has changed out of all recognition. The chimneys and the mills shown in the 1933 aerial view appear today to be of another place.

Isaac Prockter's Vale Mill however still stands and has found another life. The old churchman would probably have been intrigued and pleased.

Vale Mill is revived

New life as Chambers Business Centre

OWNERS Mohammed Yousaf (left) and Adnan Yousaf flank Ian Shepherd outside the sprawling Chambers site.

A MULTI-MILLION pound project to transform the Vale Mill at Hollinwood into a business centre is underway.

Empty since January, 2006, when the last occupiers, wallpaper manufacturers Stanley Holmes Ltd. entered into administration, the mill, at the junction of Chamber Road and Chapel Road, has been purchased from the receivers by CR Ltd., a Burnley-based property developer.

Owned by managing director Mohammed Yousaf and his son Adnan, a chartered building surveyor, CR Ltd. has been active for a number of years in central Lancashire.

The business has established itself in the residential property market and the venture at Hollinwood is the first into the commercial sector.

Built in 1868 and extended in twice — in 1882 and as recently as 1920 — Vale Mill ceased cotton spinning in 1946 and became home to the wallpaper industry and an engineering business.

The sprawling buildings, incorporating a small building which was once one of Oldham's early schools, stand on a four-and-a-half acre site and the new owners have already undertaken some demolition of extensions and lean-tos.

Now named Chambers Business Centre, all the currently available space is let with a government training agency in Progress House, what was the former design studios and an IT recruitment business in the old showrooms, now named Barclay House (see story on facing page). Both are stand alone buildings.

Completion

A legal practice has relocated from central Manchester into the mill's main offices and a design agency has taken space on the first floor of the reception area.

Work to create office space on two floors is nearing completion and, according to Ian Shepherd, who has extensive experience of business centres in Oldham having worked at Hollinwood's former Albert Mill project and the Saddleworth Business Centre centred on the Lumb Mill in Delph,

inquiries are at a high level.

Mr Shepherd, who lives in Delph, owns FM Security UK, a company specialising in lettings and management. He has been acting as an adviser to CR Ltd. and told me: "If all the inquiries firm up then we shall have all the offices occupied as soon as they become available.

"This is an excellent site, close to M60 motorway yet outside the proposed congestion charge boundary. There is ample parking on site."

He expects the next tranche of lettable space — nine offices on two floors — to be available by the beginning of September, when a new communal reception and meeting room will also be complete.

During a tour of the 165,000 sq ft former cotton mill, owner Mohammed Yousaf spoke of his plans for the site, saying: "I used

to come here to buy wallpaper and when the liquidators moved in I jumped at the chance to buy the premises.

"Everything is being done to the highest standards — state-of-the-art telecommunications and data networks, broadband, conference and meeting rooms.

"The site will be covered by CCTV and on-site security and management staff."

Once the current refurbishment works are complete, the team will turn its attention to the 90,000 sq ft on three floors of the old warehouse and manufacturing site.

A number of options are available to the developers though they are hoping that demand will drive the next set of works.

"We can create the space that tenants require," said Mr Shepherd who added that one of the options was a self-storage business.

69. New life for Vale Mill, Hollinwood (*OEC* 27 August 2008)

Appendix I

Dates of Significant Deaths

1872	Bartholomew Prockter
16 June 1889	William Mannock
24 March 1916	Ralph Holden
15 November 1916	Isaac Prockter
20 June 1919	James Stott
8 March 1924	Mrs Alice Green Holden (née Mannock) (widow of Ralph Holden)
11 September 1931	Sarah Elizabeth Mannock
4 August 1932	Mrs Mary Ellen Prockter (née Mannock) (widow of Isaac Prockter)
25 December 1933	John Holden
17 May 1941	Charlotte Mary May Prockter
5 September 1941	Mrs Ethel Sumner Holden (née Prockter) (widow of John Holden)
11 August 1946	Robert (Bob) Holden
9 April 1956	William (Willie) Mannock Holden
21 December 1963	Alice Maud Mellodew (née Holden)
26 May 1968	Gertrude Parker (née Holden)
1970	Isaac Prockter Holden
1974	John (Jack) Holden
2 March 1978	John Vernon Holden

Schedule of Dividends

S CHEDULE OF DIVIDENDS PAID on the Kirkham & Mannock Limited Ordinary Shares of £1 each, fully paid (or the subsequent ordinary shares in Kirkham & Mannock (Holdings) Limited)

N/A indicates no accounts available.

Year to 5 April Amount paid per share (converted from pre-Decimal currency)

1924	19.5p	1945	15p
1925	N/A	1946	15p
1926	25p	1947	13.63p
1927	25p	1948	16.25
1928	N/A	1949	12.5p
1929	18.75p	1950	15p
1930	18.75p	1951	15p
1931	19.35p	1952	15p
1932	16.34p	1953	N/A
1933	13.33p	1954	N/A
1934	13.33p	1955	N/A
1935	9.67p	1956	15p
1936	6.45p	1957	15p
1937	6.55p		
1938	13.33p		
1939	13.79p		
1940	16.04p		
1941	16.67p		
1942	20p		
1943	15p		
1944	15p		

Bibliography

[OLSA indicates material held at Oldham Local Studies and Archives, 84 Union Street, Oldham OL1 1DN. Tel (2016) 0161-770-4654]

Bateson, Hartley *A Centenary History of Oldham* (Oldham County Borough Council, 1949)

Bowker, B. *Lancashire under the Hammer* (Hogarth Press: London, 1928)

Bradley, Helen *Miss Carter came with us* (Jonathan Cape: London, 1973)

Dainty, Barry *The Parish Church of Saint Margaret of Antioch, Hollinwood, Oldham. A short history* (Barry Dainty 1996)

Farnie, Douglas A. 'The Metropolis of Cotton Spinning, Machine Making and Mill Building', in Duncan Gurr and Julian Hunt, *The Cotton Mills of Oldham* (Oldham Education and Leisure Services 1985; revised edition 1998)

Farnie, Douglas A. *The English Cotton Industry and the World Market 1815–1896* (Clarendon Press: Oxford, 1979)

Grace's Guide to British Industrial History 1891 (see http://www.gracesguide.co.uk/1891_Cotton_Mills_in_Manchester_and_Salford)

Gurr, Duncan and Julian Hunt *The Cotton Mills of Oldham* (Oldham Education and Leisure Services 1985; revised edition 1998)

Hansard, *Parliamentary Reports* 1959 and 1960

Hartley, William M. *An Oldham Velvet Dynasty: The Mellodews of Moorside* (Palatine Books: Lancaster, 2009) ISBN 978-1-874181-64-4

Hartley, William M. *No Longer Shopkeepers: a Hartley Family Progression* (published privately – copy at Portico Library, Manchester) ISBN 978-1-904244-51-6

Kelly's *Directory of Oldham* – 1901, 1905, 1924 (OLSA)

Law, Brian R. *Oldham, Brave Oldham: An illustrated history of Oldham* (Oldham Council: Oldham, 1999)

Oldham Master Cotton Spinners' and Manufacturers' Association – year books

Pigot's *Directory of Oldham* – 1838 (OLSA)

Reach, Angus Bethune *Manchester and the Textile Districts in 1849* (ed. C. Aspin, 1972) (copy at The Portico Library, Manchester)

Rose, M. (ed.) *The Lancashire Cotton Industry, a history since 1700* (Lancashire County Books: Preston, 1996)

Slater's *Directory of Oldham* – 1843, 1861, 1891, 1895 (OLSA)

Shiloh Spinners Limited *The Shiloh Story 1874–1974* (Shiloh Spinners: Oldham, 1974)

Southall, Derek J. *Voices of Oldham* (The History Press, reprinted 2012)

Streat, Sir Raymond 'The State of affairs in the Cotton Industry today'. Address given at The Cotton Board Conference, Harrogate 1953 (The Cotton Board, 1953)

Wilson, John F. (ed.) *King Cotton: A tribute to Douglas A. Farnie* (Crucible Books: Lancaster, 2009)

Woodruff, William *The Road to Nab End* (Abacus, 2002)

Worrall, John *The Lancashire Textile Industry* (Oldham, 1963)

Worrall's *Directory of Oldham* – 1871, 1884, 1888/9 (OLSA)

The Mellodew papers, relating patents, patterns, title deeds and cloth samples are now lodged at OLSA

Other material is contained in census returns, the wills and grants of probate (being records in the public domain) of the persons mentioned in the text, private estate and trust accounts of the same, and from personal recollections of members of the Holden and Stott families.

Index

Note. References to Kirkham & Mannock Limited and to Oldham are not listed in the Index as they form such an integral part of the subject matter of the book.

The names of females who married are listed under their maiden name, with a cross reference to their married name where page details are given.

Where a place or person is named once (such as a child who died in infancy) the place or name is not indexed, unless the place or person is important to this history.